T H E

PHILOSOPHER'S

S T O N E

THE PHILOSOPHER'S STONE

CHAOS, SYNCHRONICITY, AND THE HIDDEN ORDER OF THE WORLD

F. DAVID PEAT

Illustrations by Alex Gordon

BANTAM BOOKS
NEW YORK · TORONTO · LONDON · SYDNEY · AUCKLAND

THE PHILOSOPHER'S STONE
A Bantam Book / August 1991

All rights reserved.
Copyright © 1991 by F. David Peat.
Cover art copyright © 1991 by Bob Peters.
Cover type and design copyright © 1991 by Kirschner
Caroff Design Inc.

BOOK DESIGN BY GRETCHEN ACHILLES

Library of Congress Cataloging-in-Publication Data

Peat, F. David, 1938-
    The philosopher's stone: chaos, synchronicity, and the
hidden order of the world / F. David Peat.
        p.   cm.
    Includes bibliographical references and index.
    ISBN 0-553-35329-2
    1. Science--Philosophy.   2. Coincidence.   3. Quantum
theory.   4. Chaotic behavior in systems.   I. Title.
Q175.P38   1991
501--dc20   91-2018
                                                        CIP

Published simultaneously in the United States and Canada

Bantam Books are published by Bantam Books, a division
of Bantam Doubleday Dell Publishing Group, Inc. Its
trademark, consisting of the words "Bantam Books" and the
portrayal of a rooster, is Registered in U.S. Patent and
Trademark Office and in other countries. Marca Registrada.
Bantam Books, 666 Fifth Avenue, New York, New York
10103.

PRINTED IN THE UNITED STATES OF AMERICA

CWO   0   9   8   7   6   5   4   3   2   1

ACKNOWLEDGMENTS

The author thanks the Canada Council for its support and encouragement in pursuing the bridge between indigenous and Western sciences and visions of the world. The author also thanks his many friends in the Indigenous Science Network.

"All my relations"

CONTENTS

▓ Chapter 6 The Heartbeat of Creation

▓ Chapter 7 The Chaotic Universe: Fractals, Intelligence, and Freedom

▓ Chapter 8 Gentle Action for a Harmonious World

▓ Endnotes   232

▓ Index   238

INTRODUCTION

This book is about a new science of the universe. It reveals a vision in which mind and matter, subjectivity and objectivity, are unified into a single whole in which every cell and atom within our bodies participate in the same creative process as the human mind and spirit. It argues that the universe is, at every level, endlessly complex and that its subtlety can never be explained fully by any theory or system of scientific investigation.

The goal of this book is to transcend the traditional boundaries and distinctions between the material or "real" world and the world of human experience by exploring the deep connection between what could be called the innerness or essence of things and their outerness, their external appearance. It also explores the nature of the wholeness of our bodies, thoughts, and feelings and the link between each one of us, our society, and the earth itself. Finally, this book seeks to reawaken the sense that the whole of nature is alive and that a deep interconnection exists between all things.

The universe is home for us all. Each of us is a living part of a limitless, creative process, and as children of the cosmos, at every instant we face both an awesome freedom and a responsibility for ourselves, for others, and for our world. If we believe in the endless subtlety and wholeness of nature, we will also see the need for a new ethic—for a radically different way for society to act. In seeing ourselves as full participators in the great dance of the world, we will no longer seek to control and exploit nature for our ends. So a radical transformation in our way of being is called for, one involving a totally new form of response, which I will discuss later under the new terms *creative suspension* and *gentle action*.

■ The Search for Meaning

At some point in our lives, each of us has sensed a quickening of experience and a remarkable feeling of intensity that seems to flood the whole world around us with meaning. It may involve a sudden vivid vision of nature, almost as if we were seeing the rocks and trees for the very first time. It may embrace some other person—perhaps a child, a spouse, or a lover. It may emerge out of the focused intensity of our work or a creative hobby. It may simply flow out of a sense of the very vibrancy of one's body and whole being or be an intense inner vision. We may sense that nature is alive—alive at all levels from the rock to the tree, from the molecule to the star.

At the instant of such an epiphany, we sense that we are touching something universal and perhaps eternal, so that the particular moment takes on a luminous character and seems to expand in time without limit. We sense that all boundaries between ourselves and the outer world vanish, for what we are experiencing lies beyond all categories and all attempts to be captured in logical thought.

Such epiphanies may occur in fleeting moments, or they may pervade the whole of a person's life. Whatever their nature, they allow us a feeling of hope and an abiding sense that the universe itself has a deep meaning. At such moments, we believe that it is indeed possible to live harmoniously with the whole earth, to feel united in mind and body, and to relate in a totally satisfying way to everything around us.

Yet science seems to deny that matter could be imbued with

meaning and significance in any objective sense of the words. The material world, we are told, functions according to fixed laws and cannot be described as being free. Moreover, every structure is ultimately reducible to something simpler, to quarks or super-strings. In such an objective, material world, there seems to be no room for subjective human values such as meaning, freedom, creativity, and significance.

Synchronicities

My earlier book *Synchronicity: The Bridge Between Matter and Mind*[1] dealt with this confrontation between the immediacy of certain human experience and the distancing effect of the various rational theories and accounts that purport to explain the world. The term *synchronicity* itself was the invention of the psychologist Carl Jung,[2] who was interested in the symbols, patterns, and experiences that transcend the boundary between matter and mind, between inner experience and exterior objectivity.

Jung pointed out, for example, that a dream can spill out into the everyday world of personal contacts and material events. Sometimes the occurrences and symbols of a dream are mirrored in the external world. A person may have a vivid dream of a disaster, for example, and a day later read the same details in a newspaper. Or certain forms seen in a dream may be recognized several days later in a landscape. An internal crisis that catalyzes a personal transformation will often be echoed in the life of some-one close to us or in some pattern of external events. It is not unusual for a psychiatrist to witness light bulbs exploding, hear knocking on doors, or observe furniture vibrating when a patient reaches a critical part of therapy. In such cases, Jung pointed out, the internal and external, the subjective and objective, reflect and inform each other.

In one real-life example, a psychologist woke from a partic-ularly distressing dream in which he was involved in a brutal murder. He attempted to analyze this dream, supposing that it referred to recent events in his own life and that, somehow, he himself must have been projected into the various characters of the dream. But no matter how much he analyzed the dream, its significance—and his personal connection to it—continued to elude him. The following day, however, he received a letter asking him to act as a consultant in a case of forensic psychiatry. The details of the murder, he discovered, were identical to those in his dream.

Another example comes from my own personal experience. I had recently met an artist who showed me a number of paintings, one of which contained a curious pattern in the upper-right-hand corner. The pattern looked like a "star map," and he explained how it had first come to him during his initial sketches for the painting and had evolved out of a map used by Pacific Islanders. He described the process by which the painting reached its final form as a sort of active dreaming, carried out while awake and working.

Some days later, I went to a gathering of indigenous people who were planning a series of canoe voyages around the Pacific Ocean. Part of the motivation for this trip came from the vision of a Native Canadian woman that had later been interpreted by a number of elders around the world. Her vision was considered to be of enormous significance and consisted in part of a map remarkably similar to the one I had seen only days earlier. In some way, this same map, which had an importance that was uniting and motivating people over half the globe, had also touched and entered into the artistic vision of an English painter living in Canada.

The Australian anthropologist A. P. Elkin has written how an Aborigine, during a normal conversation or activity, may suddenly experience an involuntary movement in part of his body.[3] The person immediately withdraws into an inner meditative state that lasts for several minutes until he senses who is "coming along," a member of his tribe perhaps, in the near future. The non-Aboriginal is often shaken when, during a long trip, an Aboriginal will announce that his father has died or that his wife has given birth to a child. But to the Aboriginals, dreams and inner promptings are as real as the telephone or radio is to us. Indeed their reality lies not so much in an everyday phenomenal world but in their connection with "dream-time," the period of ancient totemic heroes that is also active in the present moment.

Jung called these connections synchronicities and suggested that they lie outside the normal confines of causality and physical law. These "acausal connections," as Jung called them, are not restricted by time or space and transcend the boundaries between mind and matter. Indeed, Jung's collaborator, physicist Wolfgang Pauli, realized that what was needed to explain them was a unification of physics and psychology—in fact, a new science that would explore what he called the objective side of human consciousness and the subjective side of matter.

The implications of Jung's ideas were explored at length in *Synchronicity: The Bridge Between Matter and Mind*, and in its final chapters, I hinted at the existence of a new science that would be able to embrace the creativity, infinite subtlety, and limitlessness of the universe. The continued unfolding of this new science is the topic of this book.

Authentic Experience

While each of us has experienced moments of intensity in our lives, when these moments of illumination have faded, we are sometimes left with a feeling of separation from the world around us. So many people, walking through the streets of a busy city, push their way through an army of strangers and avert their eyes from people begging or sleeping in shop doorways. In a crowded elevator, we create a private space around ourselves and establish a protective territory in our offices. At times, our particular profession may seem to have little meaning or to be nothing more than an endless race for promotion, status, power, and authority. Life for some of us has little true meaning or goal.

The whole question of this inauthenticity of human existence in our modern age has been explored by many thinkers and writers, particularly by the existentialists, whose attitudes have spread throughout our society. The Danish philosopher Søren Kierkegaard suggested that true individual freedom can only result in this meaningless or "absurd" universe by taking a leap into the unknown, by individual action taken in spite of its meaninglessness. For Jean-Paul Sartre, the prospect was bleaker. Antoine Roquentin, the central character in his novel *La Nausée (Nausea)*, is distanced from all experience and overwhelmed by a violent feeling of disgust at the meaninglessness of existence. For Sartre, the material world, "being in-itself" *(l'en-soi)*, is "without reason for being, without any relation to another being, being in-itself is gratuitous for all eternity," and he felt it would be futile to seek values or ethics within such a meaningless world. Yet both Sartre and Kierkegaard saw the possibility of individual freedom through an acceptance of the absurdity of life. Indeed, some people can find courage and even a certain pride in facing an empty existence, for the meaning of life can then be constructed through one's actions and decisions.

Woody Allen's *Crimes and Misdemeanors* provides a more recent popular statement of this position. In this film, the central character is driven to instigate a murder in order to hold his family and comfortable life together. Following the crime, he experiences a torment of guilt in the face of his newfound belief in an all-seeing God and a moral and meaningful universe, whose absolute law he has transgressed. Several months later, after the murder, however, he wakes to find that his guilt has vanished along with his belief in an ever-watchful God, an absolute moral law, and meaning in the universe that lies beyond that personal comfort found within human relationships and the freedom to act and make decisions.

Clearly, such attitudes reject synchronicity as a meaningless illusion and reduce epiphanies to nothing more than striking interior experiences that cannot claim validity outside themselves. But the danger in such an approach is that it can distance us from ourselves and from others, indeed from the whole of nature. It can create values and attitudes that become centered within the individual alone, or in some abstract vision of society, with no sense of participation within a much wider web of life, or belonging to a greater whole.

In its extreme form, therefore, this sense of separation spreads its dark depression over everything. Even one's own body can eventually become silent and remote. It is fed; it is washed and clothed; it becomes ill and registers pain; but it is a foreign object that can be ignored until it fails or breaks down. This distancing from one's body and all its feelings, sensations, and experiences can spread out until it encompasses the world of family and friends, natural surroundings, the planet, and even the whole cosmos. This sense of separation spreads through everything our society creates—its policies, attitudes, movements, reactions, legislations, projections, organizations, institutions, businesses, and governments.

It is of key importance to realize that talking about synchronicity, or meaning in the universe, is not a mere academic enquiry, for it vitally affects the lives of each one of us and, indeed, the survival of the planet. If we truly feel ourselves to be a part of a meaningful nature, and if there is indeed a connection between the worlds of inner experience and external events, then we will think and act in totally different ways. But what hope can there be for us if we believe that the universe has no intrinsic meaning and that all that exists is nothing more than inanimate matter following the directives of impersonal laws?

This book is a journey into the heart of what I believe is a living universe. Its vision of meaning and connection requires a new science of wholeness and creativity. So let us begin this journey and, as with all journeys, arm ourselves with maps to help us orient ourselves and discover our way.

CHAPTER
ONE

MAPS AND JOURNEYS

The search for a new physics and a new scientific vision may help to heal the wounds dividing us from nature and to reanimate our lives and society. To undertake this journey toward such a new vision, we must first reject one set of maps, those of Newtonian science, for another, which will be called nonunitary physics. But what exactly is a map? It is, in a sense, a true synchronicity, for it is a symbol of the connection between physical events in the external world and the inner life of a person or group. To view a map in this way may seem a little strange at first, but we have to remember that the road maps we use to find our way in the city represent only one very restricted example taken from the whole world of maps. Maps, to many people, are sacred objects in themselves; indeed, some societies have an absolute law that prevents the wrong person from looking at certain maps. A person who goes against this taboo is punished with death.

Moments of meaning and wholeness have become so rare within our culture that we have had to invent special words to describe them, such as *synchronicity* or *epiphany*. Psychologist Abraham Maslow[1] also referred to what he called "peak experiences." Yet, for some peoples, life is always lived at this level. So it is to these indigenous peoples, and their feeling of a direct relationship with nature, that we turn for our first map.

In the words of Chief Seattle[2] (Seathl) of the Duwamish

people of Puget Sound, "Every space, every humming bee, every part of the Earth" is sacred. Writing in the midnineteenth century, he explained, "We are part of the Earth and the Earth is part of us. The fragrant flowers are our sisters. The reindeer, the horse, the great eagle are our brothers. The rocky heights, the foamy crests of waves in the river, the sap of meadow flowers, the body heat of the pony—and of human beings—all belong to the same family."

To the Native person, everything is alive, and it is possible to talk to animals, trees, and even rocks. The idea of Jung's "meaningful connection" or "acausal connecting principle" becomes a lived experience rather than some theoretical idea. Indeed many such peoples already possess a deep and sophisticated account of their relationship to the cosmos that, in my opinion, goes beyond even Jung's approach. But to many of us, with our rational conception of nature, the possibility of communicating with inanimate matter would be dismissed as being totally out of the question. Communication, as we see it, must always involve some sort of interaction in which a signal, involving matter or energy, passes from one location to another. How, then, could a rock speak or a tree listen?

But suppose that there are other ways of being—ways in which communication becomes communion, a direct and unmediated presence? To the North American forest and woodland dwellers, this is called *skanagoah* and is the electrifying awareness of unity and balance felt in nature. When there is no separation to be bridged, it becomes possible to talk to the rocks and trees and to hear their inner voices; indeed, it becomes possible to experience the authenticity of all things. In the words of another Native elder: "We have to understand the nature. That is why we have to talk to them. We don't pray to them. We talk to them because they breathe the same air we do. We are put here with them. We are also a part of the plant life. We are always growing. We have to have strong roots."[3]

The North American continent appeared boundless to the early settlers who arrived from Europe. Yet to Chief Seattle, writing in the midnineteenth century, the White Man's separation from nature and its implications were crystal clear: "To him, one piece of land is much like another. . . . The Earth is not his friend but his enemy, and when he has conquered it, he moves on. . . . His hunger will eat the Earth bare and leave only a desert."

I believe that despite society's prevailing sense of separation and alienation, we can still capture that earlier sense of wholeness. Indeed, if we go back far enough, we are all, in a sense, indigenous people and our childhoods were flooded with a similar intensity.

A World of Maps

The Micronesians use maps consisting of sticks and small stones in their canoe journeys between the Pacific Islands. The Hopi use marks and paintings to represent their journeys across the length and breadth of the Americas; they symbolize their arrival on this continent via a series of stepping stones placed across the Pacific waters. The Ojibway have recorded their migrations and origin on sacred birch bark scrolls. Architecture and very physical arrangements of the Maori great houses or *marae* are maps of the cosmos and representations of the human body.

Navaho sand paintings, which are so sacred that they must be destroyed after use, are synchronicities because the maps themselves are sources of power. In healing, for example, the sick person journeys into the map itself by carefully walking inside its patterns and so regaining harmony with the cosmos.

Australian Aborigines make beautiful maps that represent the routes taken by The Ancestors during the period of The Dreaming in which the continent and all its features were laid down. Such maps represent the intersection and celebration of many, many layers of meaning and function. In one sense, they are representations of the geography and topography of a certain area and an expression of the relationship of society to the landscape. They are also a cosmology and a history of a whole people and their land. And most important, these maps are a walk through life for each individual Aborigine, who is on a journey from that first quickening within the womb to his or her moment of death. Every point in the landscape corresponds to part of a dream track on the map, and each region of that map has its own song lines that must be sung on certain journeys. Finally, as death approaches, each person takes a journey in order to arrive at that special region of the landscape made sacred by The Ancestor who was responsible for his or her first breath of life. In some cases a dream track may extend many hundreds of miles and pass through the territories of different tribes. In this sense a sacred story may be six hundred miles long! And so through the great journeyings within the map, the harmony of the universe, the landscape, and the individual is maintained.

Many Native Americans speak of having "a map in the head"—of being able to trace their way through their land even to the point of re-creating the great journeys of their grandfathers and grandmothers.[4] Such maps contain the memories and locations of hunting trails and the passage of game. They are also celebrations, stories of the land in all its seasons, the history of the tribe, and knowledge of its sacred places. The map is the wind in the trees and the voice of the rocks that comes into being as the child sits around the fire listening to the stories and songs of the elders. It is colored and enriched by ceremonies and journeys and expresses the feeling of oneness with plants and animals. It points to the path taken by the tribe and each member's journey through life. In some cases, as with the Ojibway Midewiwin (medicine) Society learning the meaning of these maps becomes part of the legality process of initiation.

In the Native map, there is no sharp distinction between space and time or between the sacred and the everyday. If the flesh of the buffalo or caribou is good medicine, then the act of eating that flesh makes a direct connection with the creative center of the earth. Everything in the map is, at one and the same time, both sacred and practical. Time and space within this map are infinitely rich, for each region has its own quality and value, and to move through the landscape is to enter into a story and a song.

Within such a map, there can be no separation, no distancing, no objectifying of the external, no sense of the other.

The gulf that exists between our Western topographical representations of certain features of the landscape and the maps of the Native American is beautifully illustrated by an incident related in Hugh Brody's *Maps and Dreams*.[5] Government hearings on a proposed pipeline in northern British Columbia were being held, and one day the commission visited a Native community. Various official presentations were given, maps were displayed by company engineers, and there were even topographical maps on which the Natives' hunting tracks and trap lines had been drawn. So far the inquiry had been grounded in Western society's vision of landscape, of ownership, and of what they took a map to mean. But as the meeting was about to close, people arrived carrying a sacred bundle that was carefully unwrapped to display a dream map.

This dream map expressed the whole meaning of that group's relationship to the landscape and to their own past. Indeed, it went further, for it was also a map used to guide the dead to the other world. As a true synchronicity, this map united heaven and earth, past and present, human and landscape, the world of dreams and the world of physical events.

According to the account given by Brody, the deeper significance of this map was lost on the members of the hearing who, after admiring it, began to pack up and leave. The Native people protested, explaining that having shown the map, it was then necessary that there should be a period of drumming and singing. The hearing members waited politely for one round of drumming and then left in their bus. The Natives continued long into the day. Clearly, the worlds represented by these two sorts of map readers could not be further apart.

The idea of a map, in its much wider sense, will therefore be used both as a metaphor and as an actual device for journeying through the ideas within this book. For just as Indigenous maps are drawn on sand, bark, stone, and skins so, too, scientific maps are created on paper out of numbers and abstract mathematics.

Just as the Native map represents a vision of the cosmos, so, too, enfolded within the maps of science are the values that our society holds about nature and ourselves.

The maps drawn by science are no longer satisfying to us. They do not bind us together and make us whole. Instead, they fragment our experience and reduce the landscape to an object. They are maps of alienation. We must seek to reanimate the maps of science and restore a sense of value and meaning to them.

New Maps for Old

Maps, symbols, mandalas, petroglyphs, and other symbolic works are used all over the world to express the link between the inner and the outer, between the self and the world, the individual and the environment. Such maps enrich us and bind us together. As we have seen, they are synchronicities, patterns of meaning and connection between the mental, spiritual, and material worlds. But in our own society one set of maps—the maps of science—have become the most powerful of all devices, overshadowing all other earlier maps and reducing them to the status of myths, legends, and "primitive" representations. Scientific maps have reached a high degree of abstraction and sophistication, but on the way they have lost their deeper meaning and connection to the world.

If we are to develop a new physics, a new ethic, and a new vision of the universe, we must first examine the maps of science and discover where they went wrong. Within this chapter, we will explore the very powerful ideas of Cartesian coordinates and with their help construct a special sort of map called *phase space*.

In order to reach this phase space map, we will move over a series of stepping stones, earlier maps that trace the path from the sacred to the abstract, from the qualitative to the quantitative.

▨ Maps and Perspectives

Although life in the Middle Ages was not always ideal, it possessed an aspect of wholeness and a sense that each person had a special place within society. Meister Eckehart referred to this as the "good life," an existence in which the quality of one's life came from inner peace rather than from exterior cravings for goods, possessions, money, and progress. In that period, the secular was not fragmented from the sacred; neither was art divided from craft.

Evidence of this can be seen in many beautifully worked objects, from illuminated manuscripts and carvings in bone and ivory to great cathedrals and paintings. When we look into these objects, we sense the same feeling for unity that is also present in Indigenous people's maps. A painting from the life of a saint is both the telling of a story and a religious celebration. Time and space are unified in such a painting, for the saint may be portrayed as being at several different points in his or her life and in physically different locations. Yet all these different elements in time and space are woven into a single tapestry.

When color is used, for example, it is not intended to be purely realistic but has a symbolic quality, as have the various objects in the painting. The painting is rich with shapes and symbols, and for those who know the tradition of its alphabet, it can be read like a book. The painting is an integration of the sacred and the secular. In one corner, a small dog is playing and a peasant lies heavily asleep with an empty wine skin at his feet. Yet nearby a miracle is taking place or God is looking down from heaven. Within the painting, each form is authentic in itself and exists in its own space. Everyday objects are executed with as much passion as is Christ on the cross. Each object, each part of the scene, has its own truth, and the whole is integrated in a marvelous way.

One senses, in such a painting, how immediate and ever present was the sacred. This is even made manifest in the way space itself is treated within, say, a crucifixion. The scene is simultaneously presented from many different viewpoints. One looks in silence into the face of Christ, jostles with the crowd at the foot of the cross, examines with microscopic clarity a clump of grass, stares down at the vast panorama below, looks up at the Madonna, and hovers above the earth in the company of God and His angels. The whole effect is almost cinematographic, for it evokes the sense that many different camera angles have been edited together as with a montage in which close-up, establishing shot, and medium shot are intercut.

The same thing can also be found within Persian miniatures, where each object exists within its own radiant space and takes on its own authentic form. By enfolding many different orders of space within the one painting, by integrating the bliss of heaven with the immediacy of a blade of grass, these early paintings become the outward expression of the integrated inner life of society.

But with the flowering of the Renaissance, this vision of a unified society in which each person had a special place was replaced by the individual as supreme arbiter and measurer of all things. In the medieval philosophy of "As above so below," a person was a harmonious image of the cosmos, but the motto of the new age became "Man is the measure of all things."

The human individual became the crown of creation, and individual human reason was the final court of appeal. The sacred was separated from the secular, and art from craft. In turn, the maps of art were transformed to express this new vision. In place of an integrated whole in which many different spaces are enfolded together, Renaissance art expresses the single, dominant vision of the great artist. In this period, we can actually see the shift from the old world to the new. And as the new paintings or new maps of the world develop, so our distancing from nature begins.

This change was made technically possible by the development of perspective by architect and sculptor Filippo Brunelleschi (1377–1446). Perspective is an invention of human reason whereby space is portrayed from a single viewpoint. In a sense, perspective makes a painting more "realistic." But it also imposes two new things: It makes space the dominant theme in a painting, and it distorts the forms and structures of objects in order to fit them into this dominant vision. For perspective is indeed a distortion; it is a falsehood, a denial of the essential indwelling of each object in favor of a single-minded, obsessive vision. It is not too far-fetched perhaps to see the dominance of science over nature as foretold in the dominance of perspective. (Plates 1, 2)

By portraying a scene—a crucifixion perhaps—from a single viewpoint, everything must now be pressed into service. Because a single, unique vision of space has triumphed, there can be no sacred, no personal, no indwelling space of things; there is simply a mathematical gloss placed over all objects—in more technical terms, the laws of projective geometry. A vase, a landscape, a human face, must all be stretched and compressed, distorted to fit the demands of perspective.

Not only has the artist, in a sense, abstracted himself or herself from being within nature, but abstract relationships in space have become the dominant quality. And with this move, something of the quality of things has vanished. From now on, our maps will begin to place their emphasis on what can be compared, measured, and quantified rather than what can be experienced and given interior value.

The development of perspective allowed artists to unify a painting not through its symbolic elements, or use of shape and color, but through space itself, by presenting the scene from a single viewpoint. But in doing this, it was necessary to distort natural shapes and forms. The image that comes to mind is that of stretching nature on a grid. And so by focusing on spatial relationships and measurements and forcing nature to conform to an abstract plan, one begins to lose contact with the more subtle cues and promptings of the natural world.

Plate 1. *The Martyrdom of Saint Sebastian*, attributed to Antonio (c. 1432–98) and Piero del Pollaiuolo (c. 1441–c. 1496). This picture is quite disturbing in its dramatic portrayal of space, for it defies the viewer to establish a single vantage point from which the actual events could be seen. One asks, for example, if the foreground is flat, for one looks down from a great height at the four archers in the immediate foreground while, only a few feet away, two more archers are above our eye line. The saint's head and torso are suspended a distance above us, yet the feet can be no more than three feet from the ground. The building on the far left appears to be only in the middle distance, yet the trees and river on the right are much farther away. The artists have deliberately chosen to unify the action within the painting rather than adhere to a slavish representation of perspective (The National Gallery, London).

Plate 2.   Carlo Crivelli (c. 1430/34–c. 1493/95). Crivelli's mannered and elaborate style exhibits an almost obsessive preoccupation with perspective in *The Annunciation with Saint Emidius* (The National Gallery, London).

▓ Grids and Racks

The idea that natural forms must be stretched on a grid and forced to conform to the single viewpoint of perspective in fact expresses very well just how perspective drawings were once made.

Figure 1.1. *Drawing* by Albrecht Dürer illustrates how an artist uses a perspective grid to create the illusion of three-dimensional space on a flat surface. Dürer's portraying of this act is itself a two-dimensional illusion of a three-dimensional scene.

Look at this etching by Albrecht Dürer (1471–1528). It portrays a perspective grid, the device by which an artist could take the most complex scene and cause it to conform to the mathematical law of perspective geometry. Perspective is based on a study of optics and the laws by which the rays of light reflected from a scene enter the pupil of the eye. By drawing on these laws, an artist can, using a grid of strings, project a scene onto a piece of paper and obtain its perspective correctly.[6]

Ironically, just as art was stretching the forms of nature on the grid of perspective, so, too, Elizabethan philosopher and statesman Francis Bacon (1561–1626) asked that the natural world be stretched on the grid of science. Bacon was the first to try to present the ideal methodology of science in his book *Novum Organum*. He argued that nature should be "bound into service" and placed on the rack and "examined" until she revealed the correct answers to our questions. (The use of the female form for nature was no accident.)[7]

The image of a grid represents another step in our journey from the richly integrated and directly experienced maps of nature toward the more abstract and quantitative maps of science. Already we see that Dürer's perspective grid presents the vision of the one-eyed man. It is a vision that is passive and objective, in which the eye does not scan the scene, the head is incapable of movement, the artist's body does not walk into the scene, and the hand will not touch and explore.

This autistic, monocular vision of the world is nowhere better displayed than in an illustration from one of the classics of nineteenth century thought, Ernst Mach's *Analysis of Sensations and the Relation of the Physical and the Psychical*.[8] Mach (1838–1916) was a physicist, philosopher, and psychologist whose writings deeply influenced the young Albert Einstein, and also led to developments in the philosophical movement called positivism. In the opinion of the psychiatrist Thomas Szasz, Mach also contributed to the development of Sigmund Freud's theories. While at the University of Prague, Mach conducted studies in experimental psychology and proposed that scientific inquiry always begins with physiological "sensations." These sense sensations are, according to Mach, the raw material out of which scientists construct their maps of nature. The best scientific theories, in his opinion, are those that take the shortest logical path between immediate sensation and theoretical conclusions. For a time, Mach's proposal became the ideal to which scientific theories aspired. Einstein himself grappled with Mach's notions and, in the end, showed that rather than being the end point in a short logical chain from sensation, a good theory should actually determine and point to the important observables within the world.

At the time, Mach's vision of science attracted a considerable following among scientists of a philosophical bent. But as Figure 1.2 illustrates, this view is singularly passive. The scientist sits in his armchair and surveys the world—or rather, the sensations

Figure 1.2.   The physicist and philosopher Ernst Mach lies upon his sofa, closes his right eye, and surveys the world—the epitome of scientific objectivity. From *Die Analyse der Empfindungen und das Verhaltnis des Physischen zum Psychischen* (Jena: Verlag von Gustav Fischer, 1886).

of the world impinge upon his eye. The eye has become the sole window into the universe; indeed, it almost appears as if Mach, the scientist, were hiding behind this eye, a homonculus within the skull looking out from that protected position. Science becomes the ultimate spectator, rather than a participator, in the richness of nature.

■ Cartesian Coordinates

The way perspective tends to objectify and quantify the world leads to one of the most far-reaching and productive inventions of all science—the coordinate system. Philosopher and mathematician René Descartes may be best known for his maxim *Cogito, ergo sum* ("I think, therefore I am"), his system of philosophy, the famous Cartesian split between mind and body, and the Newtonian-Cartesian system of science. But, in fact, one of his more remarkable inventions was a mathematical system of coordinates whereby any point in space can be rationally represented and every material object associated with a set of numbers that become its dynamic essence. Thanks to Cartesian coordinates, everything from quantum superstrings and the theory of relativity to map references and the tracking of satellites has been made possible. Cartesian coordinates were one of the first inventions of modern science and remain at its forefront today, for they have successfully survived every scientific revolution.

A Cartesian coordinate grid looks identical to the perspective grid of Dürer's etching. In both cases, an arrangement of parallel lines and intersections acts to define the position of an object in space. In Descartes's case, however, this grid was abstract and mathematical. Imagine that a grid is laid down on your kitchen floor (Figure 1.3). The effect will be somewhat like a system of tiles, and it is possible to define the position of, say, a bucket by indicating which tile the bucket is standing on—four tiles up from a corner and two tiles up. By treating the tiles as a coordinate grid and counting along the two walls, it is possible to describe the position of the bucket in terms of two numbers called its x and y coordinates (Figure 1.4).

Likewise, the coordinate grid can be generalized to three dimensions so that any point, anywhere in the universe, becomes

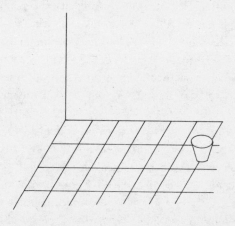

Figure 1.3. The position of a bucket on a tiled floor can be defined by counting so many tiles from the two walls.

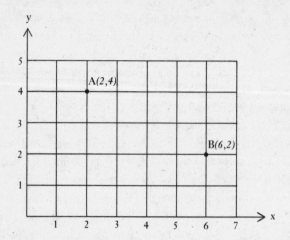

Figure 1.4. A Cartesian grid. Distances are measured along the x- and y-axes. The point A on the grid has coordinates (2,4); B has coordinates (6,2).

associated with a trio of numbers (its x,y,z coordinates) (Figure 1.5).

This Cartesian grid, along with its coordinate system, becomes the new, objective, scientific way of portraying space, and the grid is nothing less than the mathematical projection of that grid of strings portrayed by Dürer. It was in fact Descartes's goal to quantify the universe fully, and he took the first step in this direction by first quantifying space. Descartes's coordinate grid has since become one of the most powerful inventions in all of science, for Cartesian coordinates now become the measure of all things.

Since a point anywhere in space is defined once its three coordinates have been given, Descartes demonstrated a perfect correspondence between real objects in space and mathematical points on an abstract coordinate grid. From this juncture onward, the universe could be quantified and objectified. But while the map in the mind for a Native person, or a medieval painting, is rich and filled with all the qualities of space, time, and ritual, the map of science has become abstract and objectified. Everything is number. From now on, science becomes trapped and isolated like Dürer's artist behind his perspective grid or Mach's passive, all-seeing eye.

In the hands of a genius like Sir Isaac Newton, Descartes's coordinate system led to the establishment of one of the most versatile maps used in science—phase space. Owing to this ability to reduce all change to mathematical operations on coordinates in phase space, our modern age became convinced of its ability to exert prediction and control. Yet as the map of science gained in power, the synchronicities and direct correspondences of older maps became diluted.

▉ Phase Space

The Cartesian grid provides scientists with a way of describing the position of a body anywhere in space. But since most objects are not stationary, it is also useful to be able to plot out their successive positions at different times. So in order to extend the power of this map or picture of science, it is necessary to bring time into the arena.

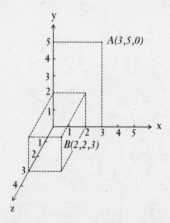

Figure 1.5.   Cartesian coordinates can also be defined in three dimensions. The point A has coordinates (3,5,0). The coordinates of B are (2,2,3).

In itself, this is quite a shocking move, for we experience time in a profoundly different way from space. Space is something we can choose to move through or to retrace. Indeed, at the end of the day, we return to the same location in space—our bed. Not so with time, for we all move through time, from past to future, and always at the same rate. Time, it seems, cannot be arrested: The past can never be revisited, and objects cannot move through time at different rates. Nevertheless, science applies a similar order of measurement to time as to space, and time is brought into the scientific map simply as another Cartesian co-ordinate. Figure 1.6 shows how an object moves to occupy different points in space at successive times.

Using Cartesian coordinates in this way enables scientists to picture how objects move in space and change in time. But even this is not enough, for this map functions purely at the level of description. Isaac Newton now had to face the central question of exactly *how* these lines should be drawn. It is a simple matter to draw a line or curve on a space-time graph. But what distinguishes a real physical trajectory from a figment of artistic imagination? What is the law of nature that governs just how these trajectories should look? What in fact determines the way bodies

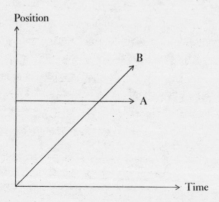

Figure 1.6. Coordinates can also be used to express distance and time. Here a body A, at rest, remains in the same position as time passes. The body B moves at constant speed.

fall through the air, move through empty space, or fly from a cannon's mouth?

Newton's great discovery was that Descartes's map had to be extended yet again—this time to include a new set of coordinates called momentum coordinates. With the help of this new set of coordinates—using both position and momentum—it became possible to uncover the law by which the paths of bodies in the universe could be drawn for any time in the distant past or the far future. With the help of this new picture, called *phase space*, the entire universe and all its activity could be mapped.[9]

For most purposes, the scientific term *momentum* can be taken as the velocity of a body multiplied by its mass. (Velocity is a combination of the speed and direction of movement of a body. So a car traveling north at thirty miles per hour has an exactly opposite momentum to one traveling south at the same speed.) Just as Descartes required three coordinates to pin down the position of a body, so Newton needed three momentum coordinates to fix a body's movement. And with six coordinates in all—three position coordinates and three momentum coordinates—it was possible to determine the complete location and motion of a body.

The new sets of coordinates demanded by Newton require a new sort of map. After all, with two coordinates, in the x and y direction, a trajectory can be drawn on a two-dimensional piece of paper. Three coordinates require the full use of three-dimensional space. But with six coordinates—three for space and three for momentum—it is necessary to draw in a six-dimensional space. Of course, such spaces do not exist in the world around us. But this should not matter, for they are abstract maps, after all, and even the shapes and colors used in everyday maps need not always correspond to reality in any direct or simplistic way. Similarly, this six-dimensional space—phase space—is a mathematical abstraction used by physicists to picture the dynamics of the world around them.

Using position and momentum coordinates, Newton was

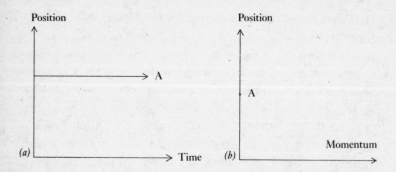

Figure 1.7. (*a*) The body A is at rest. It remains in the same position as time passes. (*b*) The momentum of A is zero.

able to create new scientific phase space maps and draw new sorts of pictures, ones in which the position, speed, and direction of movement of a body are shown at every instant. He was now in the position to question what laws govern such pictures, what fundamental truths of nature determine the way bodies move. The answer, Newton discovered, is that the primary law of natural movement turns out to be one of habit. More specifically, Newton's First Law of Motion dictates that the momentum of a body is unchanged unless it is acted on by some external force.

Constant momentum means that while position may change, the speed and direction of motion of a free body can never change. An object far out in space and away from any influence will either remain at rest or travel at constant speed, and it will continue to do this forever. In other words, its momentum will never change. This law of the persistence of momentum gave Newton his first rule for drawing trajectories in space.

In Figure 1.7, body A is at zero momentum and a fixed location in space. Since its momentum cannot change, it will remain exactly where it is, throughout all time. It is represented by a fixed point A, in phase space. Figure 1.8 shows another body, B, moving far out in space and changing its position from moment to moment. But its momentum (i.e., its velocity) is constant, so that its motion must be represented by the straight line

B. Its position constantly changes in a regular way, but its momentum remains always the same. In technical terms, its trajectory must be parallel to the position axis.

But Newton realized that here on earth things sometimes do not work in this simple way. An apple, so the story goes, had once fallen on the great scientist's head. According to the First Law, the apple should have continued to remain at rest. But this apple had begun to fall and changed its momentum from being at rest (zero momentum) to moving ever faster toward Newton's head (increasing momentum). Under what circumstances is the First Law violated, allowing momentum to change and new sets of trajectories in phase space to be generated?

Newton knew that a rock thrown across an icy pond eventually comes to rest. He also realized that this slowing down or change of momentum is the result of external contingencies, friction and air resistance. Motion in empty space involves an unchanging momentum, but when that motion comes under other influences, such as gravity, friction, or air resistance, momentum appears to change. What was needed was another law, one that dealt with these important exceptions to the First Law.

Newton's Second Law tells us that if momentum changes, it does so because somewhere a force is acting on it. Indeed, it shows that the rate of change of momentum is actually equal to the force. So with a constant force, momentum changes in a

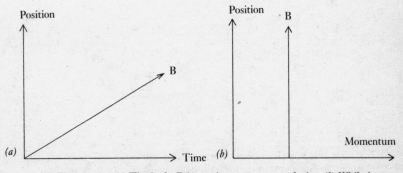

Figure 1.8. (a) The body B is moving at constant velocity. (b) While its position changes in a uniform way its momentum is constant.

habitual way (see Figures 1.9 and 1.10). In Figure 1.10, body C is acted on by a constant force that changes its momentum (velocity) by exactly the same amount each second. In other words, the body experiences a constant acceleration, which is represented by sloping line C.

Given the potential complexity of the universe, it is truly remarkable that the motion of a body can be pictured in such a simple way in terms of paths in phase space. Newton's laws tell us exactly how to draw these paths. And what is so striking about this is that starting with just one point—the initial position and momentum of a body—it is possible to draw its entire trajectory, that is, to predict its entire future.

For example, a physicist who measured the position and velocity of Halley's comet back in the eighteenth century could use Newton's laws to determine the exact date at which that comet would reappear for any century in the future. Indeed, knowing the coordinates of the sun, earth, and moon in phase space, it becomes possible to predict lunar and solar eclipses for centuries ahead. No wonder that the phase space picture was to become the paradigm of the power of science.

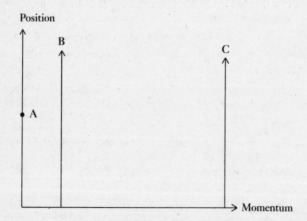

Figure 1.9. Three different cases are depicted on the phase space diagram. In A, the body is at rest with fixed position and zero momentum. In B, it moves slowly with a fixed, constant velocity. In C, it moves more rapidly with a constant velocity and momentum.

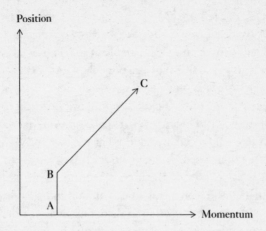

Figure 1.10. In this phase space diagram a body moves between A and B at constant velocity and with a fixed momentum. At B it is accelerated in a uniform way so that its momentum increases.

But the predictive power of Newton's new map also meant that other, older maps were rejected and forgotten. Until the rise of science, the natural world had been something in which we were totally immersed. It was something experienced by the body and spirit directly, every second of the day. The world was delight, pain, and sensation. It was something to be seen and touched and tasted and smelled and listened to, and this total involvement in the flavor and value of experience was reflected in maps, ceremonies, and symbols. Yet a new map had now been developed in which the world was objectified and made abstract. What room is there in such a map for the interior voices and quality of things when everything is quantity and number?

Let us consider, for example, the way in which physicists have viewed one of the most important symbols in the world's cultures: the moon. Astrologers have proposed that the moon affects the human personality. Poets have contemplated its changing face, and lovers have sworn on it. Indeed, the moon can be characterized in a host of ways, by its shape and the details of its geography, its color, its phases, its mass, its speed of rotation, its radius, its density, its distance from the earth, the composition of its rocks, the temperature of its surface. Each of these characteristics could, of course, be described and quantified and made to play the role of a numerical variable in some physical equation. But what, out of all this mass of possible data, is the key to the moon's motion? Is it the moon's density, its radius, its visual appearance, its magnetic field, the composition of its rocks, its mass that causes it to move in a particular way? What data about the moon have to be retained and what thrown away? This was the task Newton faced. This great scientist was also a serious alchemist who believed in the inner life of the elements.[10] Yet he realized that all these other qualities—important in different contexts—could now be forgotten in depicting motion, for Newton needed only to move to a phase space picture in which everything has been stripped down and all appearances have been reduced to position, momentum, and the external application of force.

In Newton's physics, the moon became nothing more than a point in phase space: a mass, a position, a speed, and a direction of motion. Is this the same "inconstant moon" on which Romeo was willing to swear his love for Juliet? In the Newtonian approach, the universe of motion is reduced to its bare bones; nature has been x-rayed and its inner dynamic essence portrayed. Newton discarded unquantifiable characteristics in order to reach a pure rendering of mechanical motion, one of the greatest triumphs of science.

But in exposing this numerical essence and in casting everything else away, something of great value has been lost: the authenticity of things in themselves. Within this new map, there is no longer a connection between inner experience and outer objectivity. Synchronicity has been banished from science. And this, as it turns out, is a particular irony, for Isaac Newton was himself sensitive to the inner life of nature and spent more of his life probing these secrets than he ever spent doing physics. With his deep and serious interest in practical alchemy and its symbolism, he must have known that the scientific map is only partial, that it can never be taken for the whole of reality and that it is just one picture to set beside many others. Yet through its extraordinary predictive power, the Newtonian-Cartesian map eventually replaced all others, and this mathematization of nature has since been taken for total reality. The flesh that once covered the bones of nature had been forgotten.

▓ The Power of Prediction

Descartes provided the basic insight that enabled new coordinate maps to be created and led to that first step in quantifying space, time, and motion. Newton, in turn, discovered the laws that enable the entire future path of a particle to be drawn out from a single point in phase space. Newton, and independently Gottfried Leibniz, also developed a powerful mathematical tool, called calculus, that enables easy calculations of the most complex trajectories in phase space to be carried out. Calculus has come to dominate all areas of science; and its natural alphabet is the coordinate system of Descartes.

This was the series of stepping stones that created the great scientific worldview that continues to dominate so much of our reasoning and attitudes today. Its success gave Western society enormous confidence in the power of reason and in its ability to deal with every event in terms of analysis, logic, theory, prediction, and control. It gave rise to the eighteenth century French mathematician Pierre-Simon Laplace's famous remark that had he stood next to God at the moment of creation, he could have predicted the entire future of the universe. For given the exact positions and momenta of every object in the universe at the instant of its creation, Laplace could, in principle, have calculated what each planet and rock—indeed, what every molecule—would be doing a billion years into the future. The universe is totally determined, Laplace argued, and with a large enough computer, every event can be accounted for.

Laplace's logic is clear, for if we know a single point in phase space, we can determine the future motion of a body and also work out how that body will collide and interact with other bodies. Given initial information about each one of a set of bodies, we can determine how they all will move and collide with each other.

A local intervention at a point in phase space, for example, a slight nudge that changes the velocity of a particle, will produce a predictably different path—in other words, a different future for that particle. This means that by applying a force at exactly the right moment and in exactly the correct place, it becomes possible to control the future. The future is determined and predictable; moreover, we can intervene and reshape it to our own ends. (Of course, there is a troublesome paradox in all this, for if the motion of every particle in the universe is determined, then so are the very processes of our own brains, so that even the decision to change the future was itself preordained.)

Nature has been objectified. Science has taught us to strip away the inessentials of nature in order to reach the essence of all movement and change. It has produced a system of knowledge that sanctifies our desire for prediction and control. No wonder the metaphors of physics were to spread out over all the sciences and into such disciplines as economics, sociology, and psychology. Rational analysis and mathematical modeling have become not simply a way of understanding the world but the tool used to control it. The phase space map introduced in this chapter has led us along the royal road toward a goal of evermore progress and to the supposed resolution of all human difficulties and problems.

▓ Implications

When nature was seen as vibrant and alive, human beings took their places among the other creatures of the world. Such a vision is gone today, at least for the world's technological societies. With its passing, we have also experienced a sense of distancing from the world and even from our own bodies. After all, if everything can be determined and predicted according to fixed mechanistic laws, then what room is there left for synchronicities, visions, and epiphanies? If nature is number, then why not quantify society and human behavior itself? All can be quantified and computed; all can be treated in terms of movement, leverage, balancing, equilibrium, flows of neurobiological energy or of money; all can be measured in terms of progress.

The goal of economics is to quantify and discover the essential variables that govern trade and prosperity and to determine their mathematical rules of change. And so there is a phase space for supply and demand, and control is established through checks and balances. There was even an attempt, by Sigmund Freud, to apply the idea of scientific equilibrium and the balancing of energy flows to the human psyche. The scientific picture of reality knows no limits.

This is the position in which so many of us find ourselves today. We pay lip service to the power of reason and to the scientific vision, yet our own interior experiences seem to deny its absolute validity. It is almost as if nature, in its playfulness, was attempting to piece through the barriers of logic with its synchronicities and moments of illumination.

The maps and paths of this book are designed to lead the reader toward a new science, a new picture of the world, and a new form of perception and living. We have begun by exploring the decline of those earlier maps or synchronistic representations of the natural world and their replacement by a highly successful system of mathematical coordinates and an abstract phase space. In the next chapter, we will explore the absolute nature of scientific law and ask if there could be alternative approaches to the universe.

CHAPTER
TWO

THE PYRAMID OF LAW

The previous chapter explained the powerful ideas of Cartesian coordinates and phase space. Using coordinates, scientists could take the scientific, quantitative measure of any piece of matter and compute all its possible motions and transformations for any time into the future. Science seemed to have arrived at a complete description of change, but even so, scientists were not content, for they demanded to know from where this phase map came. What was its origin? What was the true source of the laws that govern change?

Science has always sought an all-embracing picture of the cosmos. And in a way, the motivation that lies behind this quest is remarkably similar to that of the Indigenous maps of the universe. The world's first peoples sought to express the essence of the world with its plants, animals, and rocks in stories, maps, and ceremonies that accounted for the creation of things and the forces and spirits present at the birth and naming of the world.

Science was similarly asking for an all-embracing story of the world, a definitive cosmology that would account for the origin of everything that is. The goal of science was nothing less than the world's first all-embracing map, an objective vision that would transcend culture and history. Such a map would both give a meaning to the universe and contain within it a set of values. Science's quest is, therefore, no distant abstraction, for through the values and perceptions it endorses, it directly influences the lives of each of us.

■ Passion and Understanding

Science seeks to understand the world we live in, and this can be done in a number of different ways. Suppose that you want to understand the way someone from a different culture thinks and acts. Your natural reaction might be to meet this person, sit down and talk, eat with him or her, go for a walk, and even help in daily work. In short, you would simply be with that person in a variety of different situations. During this time, you would exercise an element of observation not only about the other person and his or her culture but also about yourself, your own prejudices, and your beliefs.

But dispassionate observation plays only one part in coming to understand another person, for you would also use intuition and a simple sharing of human warmth. Mutual respect, friendship, love, sympathy, humor, physical hardship, and at times, even some anger and aggression would all come into play. Indeed, observation would finally give way to the completeness of a relationship.

The activity whereby two people come into a harmonious relationship is a metaphor for the very deepest form of science, a science that seeks communion with the natural world through respect, love, and gentleness. In such a science, there can be no definitive end result or sense of finality, for in entering into communion with the natural world, we also learn about ourselves and engage in a pure celebration of our being in the world.

But there is also another, more mechanistic road to understanding. If you want to teach someone how an automobile works, what better way than having him or her strip it down, take it apart, and see how each of its components functions and fits together. Machines and mechanical structures are composed of smaller component parts, each with its own special role to play, each with its unique relationship to the other parts. The physical and mental analysis involved in breaking things into smaller pieces can be a powerful tool in gaining practical knowledge and understanding.

In fact, these two approaches—observant analysis and compassionate coexistence—could be thought of as different ends of a spectrum. After all, every skilled mechanic also has an intuitive "feel" for a complex machine, whereas a sensitive anthropologist still analyzes the structural relationships within a culture. Ideally, we move between these extremes according to the overall context of the question we are attempting to answer. Our first reaction on meeting another human being, for example, is not to jump into a structural analysis of his or her complex societal relationships. But faced with a broken lawn mower, it would be a good idea to begin by taking it apart.

Breaking things down into their component parts may work well with machines, but its effectiveness is limited when it comes to comprehending the full range of phenomena in the natural world. Physics, however, particularly in the last few decades, has shown a strong tendency to break things apart in order to reach a hypothetical, most-basic level of matter and to formulate the ultimate equation that supposedly governs the behavior of the world.

This chapter will examine this assumption of physical science and suggest a radically different way of looking at the universe. It will move toward an alternative explanation of the laws of physics. The new insights of this chapter will help us in our search for a new and more meaningful way of relating to the natural world.

■ Ultimate Explanations

While all great scientists have attempted to uncover ever more profound theories of the universe, physicists have believed that they could reach a practical understanding of the ultimate theory of reality only within our own time, and particularly within the last decade. Theoretical physicist Stephen Hawking suggested in a lecture that by the end of this century physics may have discovered the ultimate equation. Given this equation, he claimed, everything—from elementary particles to the structure of the entire universe with its myriad stars and galaxies—could be deduced.

The idea that such an ultimate equation could exist seems almost magical and, like the philosopher's stone of old, would represent the final goal in the quest of science—the ultimate answer. But is such a quest realistic? What would it mean to discover this ultimate equation? Would this represent the end of physics? These are troubling questions, for they suggest that rather than seeking to deepen our relationship to nature with all its infinite complexity, physics is really trying to discern the smallest cogs within some giant machine, to pin nature to a grid. So that we can understand the prevailing way in which contemporary physicists view nature, let us go back to the turn of this century.

■ From Atoms to Superstrings

The belief that a basic order and unity exist within the diversity of nature goes back to the ancient Greeks and beyond. Since appearances are ever changing and transformations are ubiquitous, classical philosophers naturally looked for something constant that lay beneath the surface of the world. One suggestion, made by the pre-Socratic philosophers, was that tiny, indivisible atoms could be found in all things. Atoms were believed to be the ground of existence, and their different movements and interrelationships would account for the wide diversity of materials and forms in the world.

This atomic theory resurfaced from time to time during the next two thousand years. At the turn of the nineteenth century, for example, John Dalton, an English chemist, proposed that chemical compounds and reactions could be explained by the way atoms combined together. Other scientists suggested that the properties of gases, including the way their volumes change under different pressures and temperatures, could be explained by assuming that they were composed of tiny, fast-moving atoms.

At the time, however, physicists were concerned with other issues and did not bother about metaphysical speculations such as invisible atoms. Indeed, philosophically inclined physicists, including Ernst Mach, argued that atoms were nothing more than intellectual fictions and should be excluded from science. The extent of this rejection of the relevance of the atomic hypothesis caused the theoretical physicist Ludwig Boltzmann to commit suicide in 1906 during a period of depression brought about by the general indifference to his most important life's work based on atomic ideas. How remarkable that the primary focus of contemporary physics should be on these same atoms and their inner structures. In fact, the quest for the ultimate atomic theory overshadows modern physics and represents the absolute level of truth against which all other sciences are measured.

This change in attitude originated in the late 1890s when the English physicist Joseph John Thomson (1856–1940) began examining the way electricity is conducted through gases. William Crookes had already discovered a curious form of radiation in gases, called cathode rays, and Thomson felt that these rays could be explained by hypothesizing the existence of tiny, electrically charged particles he called electrons. Thomson repeated his observations using different gases and found evidence of the same submicroscopic particles. He concluded that electrons were universal elements within the atoms of every sort of matter. Today, we know that these tiny electrons form the outer environment of all atoms. But Thomson had suddenly transformed Mach's figments of the imagination into something amenable to physical analysis. From then on, physics would be committed to revealing the ultimate level of matter.

In the first years of the present century, Ernest Rutherford directed his attention to the inner region of the atom and discovered that it contains a tiny core called a nucleus. Soon this core itself would be split into smaller parts called the proton and neutron by Rutherford and Sir James Chadwick, respectively. In the first decades of this century, it looked as if the dream of the pre-Socratic philosophers had become a concrete reality, for the whole universe appeared to be composed of electrons, protons, and neutrons.

As physicists began to probe even deeper, however, they discovered that these particles, too, had their own inner structure and could be transformed into yet other particles. From decade to decade, ever more particles were discovered and added until the list has reached the point where there are more than one hundred of them. More particles exist than different chemical elements, of which there are only 107.

This was an unsettling discovery, for scientists had supposed that the underlying structure of atoms must be the simplest possible. After all, the whole theoretical point of atoms was to provide unity within diversity. Physicists believed that the more they probed the atom, the closer they would approach some simple, ultimate level of matter.

Because of the complexity of the elementary particles, scientists began to wonder if they are really composites of even more basic entities called quarks. At first the idea was appealing, but the more this theory was examined, the more complicated it became. No one, for example, was ever able to detect a quark, and indeed, the theory itself suggested that isolated quarks could not even exist, as it was generally believed that quarks cannot be separated and that only combinations of them that make up the elementary particles can be seen.

A more recent step has been the theory of superstrings proposed by Michael B. Green, John H. Schwarz, Edward Witten, and a number of other physicists.[1] This theory argues that elementary particles are really not composed of smaller particles but that the structures of the universe emerge out of the vibrations and interactions of incredibly tiny, extended quantum entities called superstrings. In the late 1980s, superstrings were hailed as "the theory of everything," for they appeared to explain not only the elementary particles themselves but the forces between them and even the structure of space-time.

As things presently stand, superstring theory is still alive, but formulating its various implications in a rigorous way has proved emormously difficult. Indeed, at times this search for the ultimate structure of matter seems to be like trying to reach the horizon: The closer one gets, the more it recedes.

So we have seen that theories of the atom have almost come full circle. Atoms began as aspects of the creative scientific imagination that sought to discover a unifying explanation within the widely differing structures and phenomena of nature. Through the work of Thomson and Rutherford, these atoms became real because while they could not be seen directly, it was possible to design experiments to probe their inner structures. But the possibility of experimentally detecting superstrings is totally remote, and as the ultimate building blocks of matter, superstrings seem to be returning to the status of Mach's "intellectual fictions" or rather to sets of variables that are found in certain fundamental equations of physics.

The problem in finding the essence of matter lies in the inaccessibility of these tiny regions of space below the atom. When Ernest Rutherford discovered that every atom has a dense central core, he did this by firing particles into the atom and measuring how they were deflected. While the majority of these particles passed through the atom undeflected, a very few hit the nucleus and bounced back. In this way, Rutherford was able to calculate the size of the nucleus using a piece of apparatus that fit his laboratory bench top.

The particles bounced back because of the force of repulsion that surrounds the nucleus. To look inside the nucleus itself, experimenters needed even faster particles—and this meant bigger particle accelerators capable of producing the energy required to speed up the particles. The first generation of accelerators fitted into the room of a large laboratory, but soon they outgrew conventional buildings. The more intensively scientists probed the interior of the nucleus and the structure of the elementary particles, the more energy they needed. Accelerators became so big that they required the electrical energy of a small town to power them and had a radius of several kilometers. But even giant accelerators cannot take us into the world of superstrings, for the gap in scale between an atomic nucleus and a superstring is as great as that between a human being and a nucleus. Physics may have come a long way in its attempt to strip down the structure of the atom, but when it comes to superstrings, we have hardly taken the first step.

Current theories suggest that truly fundamental processes of the universe occur within incredibly tiny regions of space, and probing those regions requires energies as large as those released in the Big Bang creation of the universe. In order to probe the ultimate levels of matter, it appears that physics would have to duplicate the very conditions that created the cosmos.

According to the current paradigm of science, each level of reality can be reduced to something that lies beneath it. And just as science journeys through the material levels from organism to cell to molecule to atom to nucleus to elementary particle, so physicists believe that the laws at one level of complexity can be explained by yet more fundamental laws that operate at the level below. Understanding the structure of a molecule necessitates knowing the laws by which electrons move under the influence of an atomic nucleus. And understanding the theory of nuclear structure at a truly fundamental level requires a comprehension of why elementary particles interact in the ways they do, why they have their own particular masses and charges.

The logical structure of science is analogous to an inverted pyramid, with theories founded on theories. Supposedly, somewhere at the bottom of this heap of theories, at the apex of the inverted pyramid, is to be found the ultimate law upon which everything else is founded. Physicists believe that such a fundamental law should also be, in some way, logically simpler, for example, formulated in a deeper and more elegant mathematical way. Indeed, the mathematics used for the deepest laws of physics would itself be more fundamental than the mathematics used for less basic laws.

The laws of physics are supposed to be founded logically on ever more fundamental laws that ultimately apply to the origin of the universe itself. Indeed, some physicists dream of going beyond creation and giving an account of the origin of this origin!

In the first embryonic interval of creation, physicists believe that the universe was totally simple and described by a law of aesthetic purity and total generality. Everything that has happened since that first moment, from the birth of atoms to the evolution of life, therefore stands as a fine detail and as the smallest ripple on the ultimate ground of primordial energy. It is almost as if the entire universe were the tiniest addition to that ultimate law.

And this in itself is a paradox, for the universe is incredibly complicated and varied in all its forms, structures, and processes. The universe is our home and our experience. It is, as we argued in the first chapter, replete with meaning. How, then, is it possible for such diversity to emerge out of the simplest of theories?

Symmetry Breaking

Physicists have attempted to resolve this paradox by proposing something called *symmetry breaking*.[2] The ultimate law of nature, they argue, the one that explains both the creation of the cosmos and the smallest intervals of space-time, is mathematically the most elegant possible, which means, among other things, that it is totally symmetrical.

We are all familiar with the symmetry of a rose, a daisy, or a snowflake. But physicists have taken the ideas of symmetry much further to include the symmetry of the mathematical equations that govern the universe itself. Spatial symmetry is only one facet of such symmetry, for there can also be symmetry between the positive and negative charges of the various elementary particles, and between other properties of the elementary particles as well. For example, in addition to negatively charged electrons, positively charged electrons, called positrons, also exist. Charge symmetry demands that apart from their opposite charges, they should otherwise be identical. Electron and positron are therefore exact images of each other reflected in the mirror of charge.

Physicists have also proposed another sort of charge, called isocharge, that is not electrical in nature but allows the proton and neutron to be mirror images of each other. But in actuality, the masses of the two particles are not exactly equal, and their reflections are not exact. Physicists interpret this to mean that at a deeper level the proton and neutron are indeed identical mirror images but that additional, less fundamental effects have somehow acted to disrupt this deeper symmetry. So what can be symmetrical at a deeper level (smaller and more energetic) can have its symmetry broken at a higher level (less energy and on a larger scale).

Physicists believe that the deeper one goes into the levels of matter, the more symmetrical the corresponding theories will become. For example, at a deep enough level, the different forces of nature become unified and identical. (These four forces include the familiar forces of gravity and electromagnetism and two forces that operate over very short distances between elementary particles, the strong nuclear force and the weak nuclear force.) At this level, the masses of the elementary particles are also equal—in fact, they should all be zero.

At the smallest distance and the highest energies, the universe should therefore be perfectly symmetrical and featureless, with no distinction between one part of space and another or between the different elementary particles and forces. The ultimate origin is without form or structure, and out of this come trees and planets, stars and symphonies. How is this possible?

Most physicists believe that the universe was created in the most highly symmetrical state, in which all possibilities are equivalent, and no one process, path, or direction was favored over any other. During its unfolding in time, however, the universe had to move in one particular direction and make an arbitrary choice of one possibility over others that had the effect of breaking symmetry.

Think of the following example: You are standing in a vast desert under a cloudy sky. Everything is featureless, the sun cannot be seen, and so there is nothing to single out one direction from any other. If the desert around you is totally symmetrical, then for you to begin a journey, a step taken in one particular direction would be as good as one taken in any other. But as soon as you take your first step, you leave a mark in the sand, and this means that one direction has been singled out from all others. From now on, the initial symmetry of the desert is broken, for out of all possible points of the compass, one of them indicates the direction of your journey. Your first step may have been taken by pure chance, but from now on, as you walk forward, every step follows, one after another, in a straight line, and any direction in the desert can be given with respect to that line of footsteps in the sand.

Potentiality has been transformed into actuality, and for this reason, the outcome has a much lower symmetry than its original featureless origin. And in breaking this original symmetry, the desert has developed a structure, since one particular direction has been picked out of all others by the trail of footsteps in the sand.

Similarly, physicists believe that following its first moment of creation the universe took a series of steps that broke the conditions of its aboriginal, most highly symmetrical state. In the first instant, all the elementary particles had the same zero mass, and all forces had the same strength. But in an interval far shorter than the blinking of an eye, the universe moved in a way that split off the force of gravity from the other forces. Next, the strong nuclear force separated itself, and by then, the elementary particles had acquired much of their mass, with electrons being much lighter than protons and neutrons. As the weak nuclear force began to split from the electromagnetic force, the proton and neutron became distinct particles. At each stage, a symmetry was broken and the universe acquired a greater degree of structure.

This is the great picture of contemporary physics, the map of science, that I want to question. It assumes that all material structures in the universe can be broken down into ever smaller and ever simpler elements and that, at some level, one will reach the end of this analysis. It holds that one must understand nature by taking it apart and gain understanding by discovering how smaller components interact.

There is great abstract beauty in such a vision. Yet it is an image of nature that leaves out value and quality. It cannot accommodate the essential or subjective nature of human experience or how we relate to the world around us. It is an account that moves through abstract but defined and limited levels according to inexorable laws, which are all subsets of a greater law. Everything that happens in this universe, including its very creation, is the unfolding of a single law. The fundamental law, it seems, is ubiquitous, for it exists even before the universe began yet it is not able to account for human consciousness or creativity.

Contemporary science has managed to produce a map of the cosmos that is enormously detailed and, from an abstract point of view, incredibly beautiful. Yet this map is without any reference to the innerness of things and cannot speak to humanity's inner needs. On the other hand, it is all we have at present to guide us in the way we view the environment and even our own physical well-being. No wonder that we sometimes feel alienated within an empty universe, for when we seek truth, we are told it can be found through a process of fragmenting the world into its component atoms and elementary particles. If we are to move toward a more holistic and healthy world, then we must discover a way of unifying the statements of objective science with our personal vision of the world, and we must do this without diluting the authenticity of either approach.

If we accept nature as infinitely rich, subtle, and irreducible, we are already moving away from the mechanistic cast of mind that has dominated science for two centuries. It would then be possible to restore the essential mystery to the world and to seek understanding within the wider framework of celebration, relationship, and respect.

▓ Inscape and Landscape

There are innumerable ways of experiencing the world, nature, or reality—call it what you will. Physics is only one of these ways, and no one is more complete or more correct than any other. Nature, I am proposing, is inexhaustibly rich. It has no final resting place, no final law, no analytical ground. And each tree, flower, atom, and individual is a manifestation of this richness and can be explored without limit. So we need a multiplicity of ways of seeing and a multiplicity of relationships between these ways.

Scientists usually approach nature in terms of what could be called *landscape*—something seen outside oneself; something to be contemplated; surfaces and exteriors, forms, shapes, and movements, to be analyzed. But to see nature in this way is to remain outside as an objective observer. And clearly the current paradigm of physics, in which matter can be broken apart into ever-smaller components and in which even the orders of physical law are constructed in a hierarchical fashion on some most-basic law, is the manifestation of a tendency to see the world as landscape.

It is also possible to see nature as *inscape*. With inscape, one attempts to enter into the heart of a thing. This involves a sense of dissolution of boundaries and of a merging of one's personal horizons with that of the object. To see the world as inscape is to believe that every thing, from tree to stone, star to atom, has its own unique being and authenticity. Inscape involves a direct experience of that inner voice.

As a young man, mystic Jakob Böhme happened to notice the reflection of sunlight on a dark pewter dish. He began to gaze at the light and experienced an inner ecstasy and the sense that he was being drawn into the heart of nature. Going outside, Böhme felt that he could see into the inner nature of the plant life around him. It was as if the grass on which he walked were lighted by an inner light, as if he were participating in the meaning of nature so that everything was an act of affirmation.

One almost senses that Heisenberg had a similar vision— yet in a quite different way—at the moment of his discovery of quantum theory. One evening, while on vacation in Helgoland, Heisenberg had an insight into some problems that had been puzzling him about an earlier theory of the atom. With great excitement, he began to work out the implications of his idea and by three o'clock in the morning had the result. "At first, I was alarmed," he relates,

> I had the feeling that, through the surface of atomic phenomena, I was looking at a strangely beautiful interior, and felt almost giddy at the thought that I now had to probe this wealth of mathematical structures nature had so generously spread out before me. I was far too excited to sleep, and so, as a new day dawned, I made for the southern tip of the island, where I had been longing to climb a rock jutting out into the sea. I now did so without too much trouble, and waited for the sun to rise.

The poet William Blake wrote: "Every Space smaller than a Globule of Man's blood opens into Eternity of which this vegetable Earth is but a shadow." While for many poets a vision of the inscape of things happens only during occasional moments of illumination, Blake himself appears to have walked through the small villages that clustered around London as if he were permanently inhabiting the inscape of the world, "for heaven stands in the innermost moving everywhere."

The poet and Jesuit priest Gerard Manley Hopkins spoke of the *instress* that flows from the inscape of things and allows us to achieve an almost mystical penetration into their essence:

> The world is charged with the grandeur of God.
> It will flame out, like shining from shook foil;
> It gathers to greatness, like the ooze of oil
> Crushed.

And again,

> And for all this, nature is never spent;
> There lives the dearest freshness deep down things;

> "God's Grandeur"

Nature, Hopkins realizes, is not spent through its outward appearance, through its landscape, for there remains the secret of its inner "dearest freshness." Through the gift of instress, it is possible to experience this deeper order and even to pass into a unity of landscape and inscape.

Landscape and inscape are particular ways of being within the world and attempting to enter into its mystery. At one extreme lies the rational, objective scientist, whereas at the other is the mystical poet. But true art does not recognize such a fragmentation and seeks the unity between inner and outer, between landscape and inscape. Indeed, the true nature of synchronicity lies within this unifying movement.

To take particular examples, painters and sculptors may have particularly intense experiences of inscape, but they are also concerned with the plastic and the concrete, with realizing this vision in a particular material form. Sculptor Henry Moore said that rather than imposing his physical energy and personal vision on a block of stone, he was essentially attempting to free the authentic form that is trapped within. In this he echoes his great predecessor, Michelangelo, who would sit with a block of marble until sunrise so that he could be present when the first rays of sun penetrated its interior and revealed its truth.

The work of these two sculptors, their creative source, represents a true integration of landscape and inscape. After all, in relying on the light of the rising sun, Michelangelo was able to penetrate through the skin of the stone in a very direct way and perceive its inner landscape of grain, stresses, colors, and faults. But within this was also enfolded its inscape, the authenticity and affirmation of the stone itself. And Michelangelo was also present to his inward voices, to his own inscape and to the landscape of his technical skills, strengths, and perceptions. So that first contact of the chisel on the face of the stone represented a synchronicity between sculptor and stone, between inner and outer, between landscape and inscape. The result for all to see and experience is a great, harmonious singing, a duet between the authentic voices of sculptor and stone. To spend time before one of these pieces is to enter into that same world of integration.

Even though I have characterized the scientist and engineer as being more concerned with the landscape of things, I believe that any truly great scientist must also be sensitive to its inscape. All great scientists are motivated by the innerness of things. As to the presence of inscape within technology, Woody Morrison, a Haida Indian, has told me about the carving of a traditional canoe and the historical processes that shaped its particular structure. Considerable technological sophistication is involved in the design and construction of the canoe, and to some extent, this can be translated into the language of Western science and engineering. Yet the understanding of the processes is also connected to an inner knowing. Knowledge of the first canoe was given to the Haida by Raven, yet Raven withheld the final form, which only evolved through centuries of being with the trees of the forest and the movement of the ocean. Ocean, wind, and tree are all alive and sing together through the finished canoe and through the technical skill and inner understanding of the Haida people. Again, the highest achievements occur when inner and outer, landscape and inscape, work together as a true synchronicity.

▓ Reality as Flux

Using that dual vision of inscape and landscape we now realize that the nature of reality—and even of matter itself—can never be exhausted by any system of investigation, nor can it be fully described through reason. This has an important consequence for the whole meaning of physical law, for it implies that there can be no most-fundamental law, nor in fact can any law be totally complete. Physical laws depend on contexts and can never have a truly universal validity that lies outside all and every context.

I want to suggest that laws, rather than being absolute proscriptions on ways of being within the cosmos, are really nothing more than an expression of the various patterns that can be found at different levels of the universe. Rather than determining the behavior of matter, physical laws are human attempts to seek a unifying description of a variety of seemingly different events by gathering them under mathematical formalism.

Viewing physical law in this way means that the deepest essence of things lies within natural objects themselves and is not imposed from outside. It means that each level is complete and that each of us retains personal sovereignty. Certainly science, medicine, and psychology may offer their explanations, and these can be of immense practical value. But in the last analysis, we ourselves are the final court of appeal over the meaning of our lives and the understanding of what our bodies are telling us.

▓ Flux and Symmetry

These new ideas about the meaning of physical law will be unfolded further in Chapter 6, but to anticipate a little, let us say that the laws themselves are patterns thrown up by the flux of the universe. Even this word *flux* itself poses a problem, for it suggests a category of existence, something that can be analyzed and described. It would be more accurate to say, perhaps, that nature emerges from what lies beyond all attempts to be pinned down; from what is beyond anything that can be expressed in terms of order, form, language, or law; from what is not conditioned in any way; from what can never be reduced to something that is more elementary. The laws of nature are, in essence, the expression of unifying patterns within an ever-changing landscape and in themselves are never absolute. Indeed, to ask for definitive laws of nature may be similar to asking for a definitive account of a work of art. Just as the meanings and interpretations of a poem or painting can never be exhausted, neither can there be an end to the probing of matter or a final theory of science.

Nature should not be viewed as a great robotic machine with rigid component parts, for it is closer to an ocean that is constantly tossing up ever different forms and patterns of waves. By observing a small region of the ocean over a limited time, one may sense a certain regularity and pattern. But quite different patterns may appear at other scales and over other time periods. So regularities and laws can always be seen within particular, limited contexts. But in a wider context, one would realize that they are part of some greater movement. Physical laws, in this sense, are no longer fundamental but simply a description of persistent patterns that appear at particular scales and within limited contexts. Law is no longer absolute but depends on the context in which nature is viewed.

The complexity of the universe does not emerge out of some underlying, most simple, formless level, as in theories of symmetry breaking. Rather, its forms appear out of complexity, like vortices from a river. That which we see as simple patterns or orders may be nothing more than a sort of averaging out, an approximation within a particular limited context, within this underlying complexity and flux. If we explore nature from within the confines presently set by conventional physics, we will indeed see what appear to be constant patterns that obey fixed laws. But if we can move beyond the boundaries of that context, we will see that the laws themselves are only provisional.

▓ Penrose and Gravity

In his investigations of the fundamental nature of gravity and space-time, mathematician and physicist Roger Penrose has made a discovery that goes some way toward supporting these ideas, for it contradicts the prevailing notion that the more fundamental the law, the more symmetrical it must be.

In describing the nature of gravity at the quantum level, Penrose uses geometric forms he calls *twistors*.[3] Following Einstein's original vision, physicists believe that the force of gravity has its ultimate origin in the geometry of space-time. The moon orbits the earth and the apple falls, Einstein argued, because the space-time in which they move is curved. Einstein's theory works perfectly in the large-scale world of apples and moons, but what happens when we reach the subatomic level of things? Gravity is a force and quantum theory dictates that all forces have a quantum origin. What, then, is the quantum curvature of space-time? This question has proved to be one of the most difficult that physics has faced in the last half of this century.

Penrose has proposed a new answer in terms of his twistor geometry. He shows how space-time curvature, that is, the force of gravity itself, emerges out of two basic types of twistor geometries—left- and right-handed curvatures. Now, according to conventional scientific wisdom, any theory that deals with the quantum nature of space-time must be coming very close to being a most fundamental theory of the universe; therefore, it should be formulated in the most simple and symmetrical way possible. In other words, the right-handed and left-handed curvatures of space-time should be essentially equivalent, with any subsequent distinction between them coming about as the result of symmetry breaking. The geometry of space-time should arise out of one law and one fundamental equation.

Penrose, however, has shown that, by contrast, the origins of the left- and right-handed curvatures are distinct; indeed, the mathematical forms that must be used to represent them are quite different. The overall curvature of space-time therefore emerges out of two quite different mathematical forms. Rather than the difference between a right- and a left-handed curvature arising through the symmetry breaking of some initially ambidextrous curvature, the reverse is true. Where space-time has a symmetrical curvature, this must have arisen out of an averaging out from underlying processes that are not symmetrical. In other words, the underlying theory is the one with less symmetry rather than vice versa!

Penrose's conclusion is remarkable, for it shows one way in which a deep description of the physical world need not be founded on a most symmetrical law. It opens the possibility that other laws of physics could have a similar unsymmetrical formulation. Once the simplicity of the most basic laws has been lost, then entirely new possibilities must be admitted. And in beginning to free ourselves from the confines of absolute physical law, we may be more able to redraw our maps of the world. But for now, we shall leave the whole nature of the laws of physics and return to them in Chapter 6.

CHAPTER
THREE

QUANTUM THEORY: FROM
DETERMINISM TO AMBIGUITY

As we have seen, the idea that matter, at all levels, is complete in itself requires the development of a whole new attitude toward physical law. In order to move toward this new vision of the world, we need to continue our journey through the maps of physics. This chapter will discuss quantum theory and show that although quantum views produce powerful insights, a approach to studying and comprehending subatomic matter is still needed.

We have seen how Newton's phase space map, with its enormous power to predict the movements of matter, has driven synchronicity out of the universe through its absolute determinism and all-embracing power of description. At first sight, quantum theory, which replaces the phase space approach, appears to offer hope for a more integrated picture of the world, but it is plagued with paradoxes that render its explanations incomplete. In seeking a new quantum theory, we must radically change the map of physics and the meaning of physical law.

Nevertheless, quantum theory has produced a revolutionary change in the way scientists think about the universe. It has, for example, called into question our habit of distancing ourselves from nature and the rigidity of the whole phase space picture. We can see one way it does this in the following simple but striking example—the double-slit experiment.

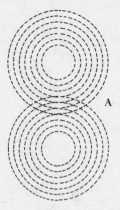

Figure 3.1. Two waves in an otherwise calm lake expand until their outer edges meet. Interference occurs within this region (A) to create strongly disturbed water.

■ The Double-Slit Experiment

A stone thrown into a calm lake causes waves to spread outward. If one of these spreading set of waves should happen to meet another, the two will interfere and interact with each other. The result is a complex pattern of wavelets. In that region where the crest of one wave meets the crest of another, the disturbance in the water level becomes even higher. Likewise, the meeting of two troughs produces a deep depression. But if a crest happens to meet a trough, the two will cancel out and leave a tiny region of flat water. In that region of the lake in which two sets of waves meet, there is therefore a complex and characteristic pattern of disturbed water

This same interference effect can be seen using ordinary light. A narrow beam of light falls on a barrier containing two narrow slits. A white screen is located behind the slits. The light that passes through the slits spreads out very slightly, like ripples on a pond. In the region where these two sets of expanding waves meet, interference of the light waves occurs. Where crests meet crests, the light becomes more intense, but where crests and

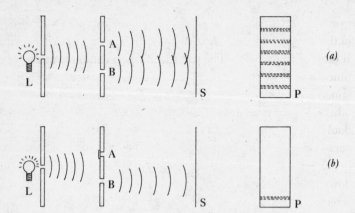

Figure 3.2. (*a*) In the double slit experiment, light from lamp L falls on two slits, A and B. The resulting light waves spread out from the narrow slits and interfere on their way toward the screen S, producing a characteristic pattern (P) of light and dark bands. (*b*) With slit A blocked, the interference pattern vanishes and a single band of light is seen on the screen.

troughs meet, light cancels out. By allowing this complex pattern of light and dark to fall on the screen, a characteristic interference pattern, of light and dark bands, is produced.

One can easily check that this phenomenon must be the result of interference by blocking one of the slits. Light waves are now able to spread from only one slit, and in place of the previous pattern of light and dark bands, there is only a single band of light located directly behind the open slit. Unblock the second slit and the original interference pattern returns

This interference pattern was interpreted by physicist Thomas Young (1773–1829) as positive evidence that light must actually travel in the form of waves. What is particularly exciting about this is that the experiment can be repeated today at the quantum level in such a way that it totally explodes the validity of the phase space map within the quantum world.

Light, as Max Planck and Albert Einstein discovered in the first years of this century, has an underlying quantum nature. Like all forms of energy, it is made up of tiny indivisible units of energy called quanta that cannot be broken down into finer parts. Probe the fine structure of light, and its quanta (also referred to as photons) are discovered. But these quanta are curious things in that they have a dual nature, behaving at times like waves and at others like particles. The particular aspect exhibited at any one time depends on the nature of the experimental observation. Certain experiments can only be explained in terms of wave motion, others only in terms of localized particles. When it comes to the double-slit experiment, however, the results are puzzling and paradoxical.

Suppose that the intensity of light falling on the slits is cut down so that it becomes weaker and weaker. The pattern on the screen fades and becomes invisible to the human eye. But if a photographic film is pinned to the screen and left for many hours, it will accumulate evidence of this very weak light. An individual photon that hits a silver atom in the emulsion will produce a change that later appears as a tiny dot when the film is developed. Expose the film for long enough in this very weak light and the accumulation of a very large number of dots shows exactly the same interference pattern as was seen with the naked eye in much brighter light.

And what if the light is cut down to the point where only a single photon falls on the screen at any one time? According to the phase space picture, this photon must follow a fixed path to the screen, the details being determined by the photon's initial position and momentum. A single photon leaves its source, taking a definite path, passes through one of the two slits, hits the screen, and is registered on the photographic film. (Of course, most photons will miss either slit and simply hit the barrier, where they are then absorbed. But we will not worry about these—only those that get through slit A or B are eventually registered on the photographic film.)

But photons leaving the light source are not all going in precisely identical directions. One may take a very slightly different path that causes it to travel through the other slit. Time and time again, individual photons shoot toward the barrier and pass through one or the other of the two slits. In this way, so the phase space picture dictates, two independent images should be

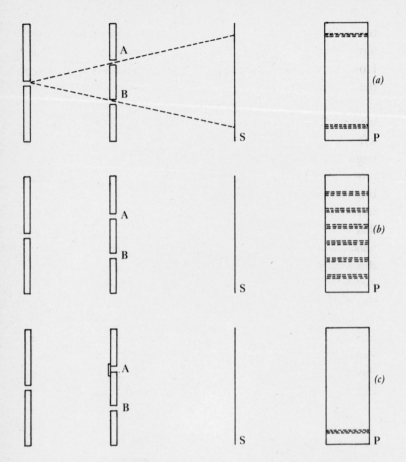

Figure 3.3. (a) If photons are really tiny corpuscles, then no interference should be possible. All that should be seen on the screen are two bands, one located behind each slit. (b) Even when photons are used one at a time, the familiar interference pattern is produced. (c) When slit A is blocked, the quantum interference pattern vanishes.

built up on the photographic film. One of these images is created when a bunch of photons hits the screen directly behind slit A. A similar image is found behind slit B.

But quantum nature holds a surprise: When the film is developed, something unexpected is seen—the familiar interference pattern is still present! Instead of two independent bands, one behind each slit, the same alternating pattern of light and dark bands appears. This means that some photons must have hit the film exactly midway between the two slits. How is this possible? How can a single photon appear in the region midway between the two slits?

When this result is checked by repeating the experiments with slit B blocked, the interference pattern vanishes, and we are left with a single band of light behind open slit A. This poses a staggering problem, for how does an individual photon going through slit A ever know if slit B is open or closed? The fact that B is open or blocked produces a totally different pattern on the screen. But how can a photon, after passing through slit A, know that if B is open, it must then curve its path so as to hit the photographic film at a point midway behind the two slits? It is almost as if the photon could be in two places at once or as if it were receiving remote information about the status of the second slit.

For two hundred years the physics of phase space has been telling us that bodies move along definite trajectories. Now the idea ceases to make sense, for an individual photon seems to know about both slits. It is almost as if the photon has interfered with itself or has been in two different places at once. Yet a basic tenet of quantum theory is that a photon cannot be split in two—it is indivisible.

It seems that the whole notion of a path must be abandoned and that some totally new sort of map must replace the phase space picture.

◼ Heisenberg's Uncertainty Principle

In the decade before Werner Karl Heisenberg's discovery of quantum theory, Niels Bohr had tried to hang on to the old phase space picture by making some modifications in the way the trajectories of quantum particles were drawn. But to Heisenberg, it seemed as if Bohr were putting old wine into new bottles. Heisenberg recognized that a total revolution, not a modification of the phase space picture, was needed.

In phase space, the future movement of any object can be fully determined, provided that at one particular instant we are able to pin it down to a point in phase space. Given its precise values of position and momentum (a point in phase space), we can predict an exact trajectory for all times in the future.

But in setting down the new quantum theory, Heisenberg realized that an absolute limit was being placed on how accurately these two coordinates—position and momentum—can be known. Heisenberg's uncertainty principle shows that if you measure the position of a body very accurately, then knowledge about its momentum becomes uncertain. Conversely, if you focus on momentum, then its position becomes uncertain. This means that it is no longer possible to pin down a quantum particle to a point in phase space. And if there is no such starting place, it will never be possible to calculate the quantum particle's path or to predict its exact future. At one stroke the whole justification for using phase space at the atomic level is thrown out of the window.

■ Quantum Measurements and Objectivity

Heisenberg's uncertainty principle, and the abandonment of phase space, comes about through the essential wholeness of all quantum phenomena and the way the observer is linked to what is observed. Whenever a scientist attempts to observe the quantum world, the experimental apparatus used must interact in some way with the quantum system. This interaction always involves at least one quantum of energy. But the quantum is indivisible, and this means that the interaction itself, the very act of observation, cannot be in any way analyzed or divided.

When you look into the heart of an atom, you are irreducibly linked to it, for both you and the atom form a single, indivisible whole. But this means that it is never possible to make compensation or adjustment for the effects of an act of observation. Every act of observation must involve some measure of disturbance, but since the quantum is indivisible and cannot be broken apart in any way, this means that it is never possible to suggest that the disturbance was generated solely by the observer, or in part by the atom.

This quantum wholeness has the effect of placing a limit on objectivity during quantum measurements. It indicates that the act of one measurement (say, position) will have an effect on a second measurement (momentum). It also means that the result of a combined measurement of position and momentum, or of some other pair of quantum variables, will always carry a measure of ambiguity.

But if the link between the observer and the observed is unanalyzable, then where exactly does "quantum reality" lie? Is it in the observed, or is it in the observer? Or does it lie in the very act of observation itself? When reality was objectified and the world placed behind a plate glass wall of phase space, it was easy to speak of seeing things in themselves and to believe that we could know the intrinsic properties of objects.

The phase space picture of the world that dominated scientific thinking for over two centuries deals with a world composed of independent objects and implies that we can separate ourselves from nature and become the objective observers of the world around us. Quantum theory, however, fundamentally rejects such an idea. The world is a whole, the theory teaches, and the observer is linked to what he or she observes. At last the observer is to be reintroduced into the map of science, and fragmentation is to be replaced by wholeness. But we must still face the question, Does quantum theory go far enough? In rejecting the rigidities of the earlier phase space map, does it have a consistent picture to set in its place?

▪ Hilbert Space

To describe the motion of an object in phase space, it is sufficient to know its position and momentum coordinates. In fact, the same thing can be done for a whole collection of particles. By extending phase space so that for each particle there are three dimensions of space and three dimensions of momentum, the state of a many-particle system can be pictured directly as a single point in space. Even the whole universe can be reduced to such a point! And to the physicist, this point *is* the state of the system, so that the correspondence between map and actuality is direct and unambiguous.

But what corresponds, in the quantum world, to this picture of points in phase space? If the state of the moon is a point in phase space, then what is the state of an electron? After all, Heisenberg had abandoned the very notion of a quantum particle as having a trajectory in space.

Physicist Erwin Schrödinger talked about quantum states in terms of what he called wave functions, and this wave function, so physicists believe, contains the most complete description of an electron, atom, or molecule possible. And remember that unlike the case of large-scale objects, there will now be a certain level of ambiguity in this description.

Just as the introduction of coordinates in Newton's physics requires an arena for their expression—phase space—so, too, a new kind of map is needed for the wave function. Physicists call this new picture Hilbert space.

It turns out that the word *space* in the term *Hilbert space* has nothing to do with our familiar notions of space as something we move around in. Neither does it have anything to do with adding extra dimensions to our everyday space. Hilbert space is, in fact, quite abstract. It so happens that mathematicians have been able to generalize some of the more formal notions of everyday space into something quite abstract. Just as the ordinary numbers we use when we count can be generalized to include imaginary, complex, and transfinite numbers, so, too, the concept of space can be generalized into something called Hilbert space.

Hilbert space was developed by the great mathematician David Hilbert, not as a tool for quantum theory but, decades earlier, as a way of studying special mathematical functions. In this mathematician's space, the basic elements are not points and coordinates but what are called vectors, that is, lines pointing in specific directions. The idea of a point in Hilbert space does not really apply only to a vector. Moreover, the dimensionality of Hilbert space depends on the particular quantum system involved. It is not the familiar three dimensions of our everyday space—dimensions range from two dimensions to an infinite number!

It turns out that every state of a quantum system, also called its wave function, can be represented by a vector in Hilbert space. To put it another way, a vector in Hilbert space—a line that points in a given direction—corresponds directly to a Schrödinger wave function. The length of these vectors does not really matter, and they could be thought of simply as arrows, for what is really important is the direction in which this arrow is pointing. An arrow pointing in one direction corresponds to a particular state of a quantum system; an arrow pointing in another direction corresponds to some other state.

Hilbert space vectors could also be compared with compass directions. One vector points north and corresponds to a particular state of a quantum system. Another points west and corresponds to a different state. At first sight, all this may seem to be nothing more than a generalization of our earlier picture in which a point in phase space has now been replaced by an arrow in Hilbert space. But, as it turns out, the two descriptions could not be further apart, for the properties of Hilbert space vectors are profoundly different from those of points in space. In fact, it is possible to add these compass directions, or vectors, together.

Suppose you head due north in a boat and then change your mind and head west. At some point, you will find yourself in

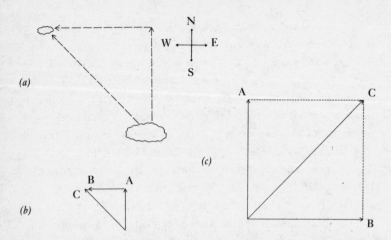

Figure 3.4. (*a*) Our traveler can reach the second desert island either by heading directly northwest or by first rowing due north and then due west. (*b*) This journey can also be expressed in terms of vectors. The vector C can be decomposed into two other vectors, A and B, that are perpendicular to each other. (*c*) The vector C can be created out of two other vectors, A and B, that are perpendicular to each other. The process of combining vectors, or decomposing them, can be carried out in any number of dimensions.

exactly the same position as if you had originally headed northwest from your starting point. As Figure 3.4 shows, add two vectors together and you get a third, a new vector. Or conversely, any vector can always be split apart into two other vectors at right angles to each other (Figure 3.5). The vector corresponding to the southeast setting is therefore equivalent to the combination of two vectors, one heading south and the other heading east.

What is true about compass settings in a two-dimensional space is also true of vectors in Hilbert space. Any single vector can be broken down into a combination of other vectors, all at right angles to each other—in fact, as many component vectors as the Hilbert space has dimensions. But this implies that the *state* of a quantum system must also be equivalent to a combination of other states. Or conversely, that many different quantum states can be combined together to produce a completely new state.

This result is certainly bizarre, for in our everyday world we are used to objects being either one thing or another—that is

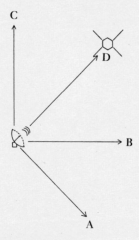

Figure 3.5. The position of the rocket is pinned down by the vector D. D can be split into three components, all at right angles to each other: A—pointing east; B—pointing north; and C—pointing directly upward.

a rock, and this is a tree. But now we are entering a world in which an object can simultaneously be both a rock and a tree, or a wave and a particle, and in which many distinctly different states can all be manifested within one single state!

This ability to blend quantum states together—and equally easily, to decompose a single state into a host of others—is a direct consequence of the Hilbert space picture that quantum theory has forced onto us. In place of the single, objective phase space picture is a description in which each state is, in part, every other state.

Let us look at the double-slit experiment again. Common sense dictates that a photon can be in only one place or another. If it passes through slit A, then it cannot, at the same time, be passing through slit B. But common sense is about to be cast aside, for there are vectors in Hilbert space that correspond to just this paradoxical situation. These vectors are combinations of (1) a vector that corresponds to the photon going through slit A plus (2) a vector that corresponds to a photon going through slit B.

Such a vector would appear to describe a photon that is in two places at once—a photon, moreover, that by the rules of quantum theory is essentially indivisible! The photon is indivisible, yet at the same time it is a combination of other vectors, states that represent a photon passing at one and the same time through different slits.

■ Schrödinger's Cat

The new quantum description, in terms of vectors in Hilbert space, is worlds away from the earlier phase space picture. On the one hand, since vectors can always be combined together, there is a basic ambiguity about quantum states. On the other hand, the equation that determines how a vector actually moves and changes its direction in Hilbert space, Schrödinger's equation, is totally deterministic. Just as knowledge of a single point in phase space is sufficient to determine every future point the system will occupy, so, too, given a vector at one instant of time enables its direction, and hence the quantum state, to be calculated for all future times.

But there is a curious paradox in this. On the one hand, the movement of Hilbert space vectors is totally deterministic; on the other hand, quantum processes such as the disintegration of an atom are probabilistic. On the one hand, quantum states are ambiguous in that they may be expressed as combinations of other states; on the other, everything we experience about the physical world is definite and free from ambiguity.

This paradoxical position was clarified by Erwin Schrödinger in his famous *cat paradox*. Imagine that a live cat is sealed up in a box in a scientist's laboratory. The box contains a quantum device that can cause the death of the cat. For example, the disintegration of a radioactive atom is registered by a Geiger counter, the output of which is then fed to a mechanical device that causes a hammer to break a flask containing cyanide (Figure 3.6).

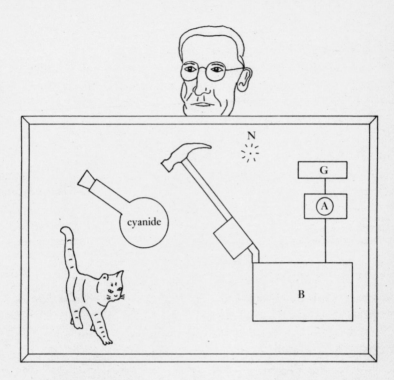

Figure 3.6.   In the Schrödinger cat experiment, the decay of a radioactive nucleus (*N*) is detected by a Geiger counter (*G*). The output is passed through an amplifier (*A*) and into the box (*B*), which activates a hammer, smashing a flask of cyanide.

The experiment is set up using a radioactive nucleus that has a fifty-fifty chance of disintegrating within, say, the next half hour. If the nucleus happens to disintegrate within that time limit, the cat will die, but if it does not, the cat will still be alive. The actual outcome is pure chance. At the end of the half hour, the box lid is opened. But just as the experimenter reaches out to raise the lid, the question is asked, Is the cat alive or dead?

In a phase space world, things are straightforward. The radioactive nucleus is replaced by another probabilistic system, a roulette wheel, which is then hooked into the system. Again, the outcome is pure chance—a fifty-fifty chance that the cat will be dead by the time the box lid is lifted. Until that instant, the fate of

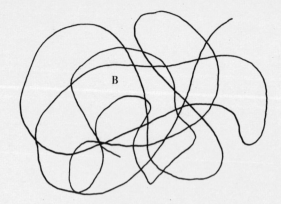

Figure 3.7. A phase space picture (really this should be drawn in very many dimensions) showing a dead cat (A) and, in a different region of phase space, the ever-changing state of a live cat (B).

the cat is totally unknown. But one thing *is* certain: The cat must either be alive or dead (Figure 3.7).

Quantum theory, however, gives a profoundly different answer. The state of any system is specified by a vector in Hilbert space, and as we know, this vector can be a combination of many other vectors. One of these vectors may correspond to a live cat and another to a dead cat. So the state of the system can correspond to a combination of these quite different outcomes. All that one can say, before the box lid is opened, is that the final state of the system is represented by all possible vectors in Hilbert space, by all possible outcomes. In fact, the instant before the experimenter reaches out to open the lid of the box, the cat is neither alive *nor* dead—it is a combination of all possibilities (Figures 3.8 and 3.9)!

Quantum theory certainly opens up a strange new world. A photon that goes through one slit while seeming to know about what is happening some distance away sounds bad enough, but a cat that is both alive and dead seems totally absurd. Yet all this follows inevitably from the ability of vectors to combine in Hilbert space. From the deterministic phase space picture to Hilbert space, the pendulum seems to have swung from absolutes to total ambiguity. The basic paradox, of course, is that we do not observe

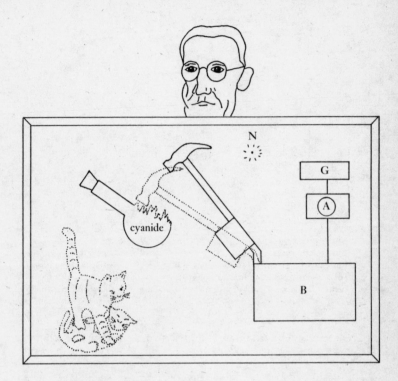

Figure 3.8. According to quantum theory, the contents of the box consists of various combinations of a live and a dead cat.

ambiguity in everyday occurrences. Indeed, when we finally open the lid of the cat's box, we know full well that we shall see either a live cat or a dead cat. Opening Schrödinger's box appears to collapse an ambiguous mixture of possibilities into a single outcome.

Physicists call the act of opening the box lid, or making any other quantum measurement, the *collapse of the wave function*. For when any measurement is made in the laboratory, the ambiguity represented by a superposition of different states or wave function always collapses into a single actuality. At this juncture, some physicists believe, quantum theory is incomplete, for it is not able to give an account of the collapse of the wave function or for the singling out of one Hilbert space vector for a combination. All measurements in our human-scaled world are definite and unambiguous—a Geiger counter clicks, a dial moves, a meter registers.

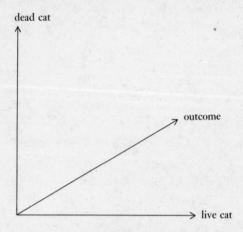

Figure 3.9. According to quantum theory, the state of the cat inside the box must be given by a superposition of different possibilities, or Hilbert space vectors. A simplified version of one possibility is given here. In reality, however, Hilbert space will have an infinite number of dimensions.

Yet all that quantum theory can offer is a superposition of many different outcomes with no way of picking out one over the other.

Quantum Interpretations

In attempting to deal with this problem, physicists have come up with a variety of suggestions.[1] All of them, however, involve some sort of assumption or mechanism that lies *outside* quantum theory itself, for the theory, taken in its pure form, has nothing to say about how actuality emerges from ambiguity. Indeed, not only do the various attempts to solve the quantum measurement problem lie outside the proper domain of quantum theory, but many of them sound farfetched.[2]

One idea is that quantum theory does not apply at the level of everyday objects, or that new sorts of interactions at the large scale cause the Hilbert space picture to break down. Quantum theory may work for electrons but not for cats. But this poses the problem of deciding exactly where one theory breaks down and another takes over. Is there a boundary at some definite level of scale, or do the two radically different theories somehow merge into each other? And what determines the nature of the inter-connection between the two theories? Does this emerge perhaps from some additional, third theory?

Another suggestion is that it is the actual human observer who causes the collapse of the wave function, for human consciousness is the missing factor in describing the world. But this leads to further paradoxes and problems. For example, does this mean that physics somehow changed at the point in evolution where consciousness first appeared? Was everything ambiguous before that moment? And has the whole universe changed? For human eyes can observe the effect of quantum processes on distant stars in the form of the light they radiate.

And what if the experimenter together with the Schrödinger box is sealed into a yet bigger box? Is the first experimenter himself or herself now a superposition of states, along with the cat? And is this ambiguity resolved when the second experimenter opens the larger box—the laboratory door? And what if this whole system is itself in a yet bigger box, and a third experimenter . . .

Other physicists have proposed that all these different states, corresponding to different combinations of Hilbert space vectors, each have a real, independent existence. But each exists within its own universe. There are, therefore, an infinity of parallel universes, each totally independent of all others. Moreover, each time a quantum measurement is made, a host of new universes must be created.

None of these explanations is really satisfying, however, and for this reason, as well as for a number of others, quantum theory must be considered as being neither satisfactory nor complete.

At first sight, quantum theory appeared to have opened new possibilities for understanding the wholeness of nature and the irreducible link that occurs during the act of observation. But now we realize that the theory is essentially incomplete. In its present form, it cannot really account for the way the world works in any satisfactory way, nor does it integrate in an entirely con-sistent way with that other great theory of modern physics—

general relativity. Clearly, something new is needed, an approach that is able to move beyond the confines of phase space but one that retains certain insights of the Hilbert space picture, which allows for the authenticity of things and offers the possibility of a fresh approach to natural law. In the following chapter, we shall step into this new region by seeing how natural systems can spontaneously evolve their own forms and structures and how the language of Hilbert space can be modified to account for this.

CHAPTER FOUR

LIFE FORMS

Conventional quantum theory demands that an atomic state be represented as a combination of different vectors in Hilbert space. Yet at our human scale of things, physicists deal quite effectively with points and trajectories drawn in phase space. How, then, do the well-defined forms of our everyday world emerge out of quantum uncertainty? This question can be illuminated by the example of a crystal.

Take a cup of salt water and place it in sunlight on a window ledge. Over the course of the day, the water in the cup evaporates, leaving tiny salt crystals around the side. It is possible to take one of these crystals, place it in a new saturated salt solution, and increase its size as the solution evaporates once again. This process can be repeated to create an ever larger crystal.

Such crystals always have a very definite form. The crystal is not ambiguous, for its properties do not depend critically on the experimental observations of an external observer. We do not suspect, for example, that the shape of a crystal changes when placed in a different experimental context. A salt crystal is an objective fact in the world.

But think of the crystal's origin. It began in the chance encounter of sodium and chlorine atoms (ions, to be more exact) within the solution. These atoms constantly collide with each other and bounce apart. But as more and more water evaporates and the concentration of salt in the solution increases, the tendency of these atoms to stick together increases.

There are many ways in which the first few atoms can arrange themselves, each of which can be represented by a vector in Hilbert space. The quantum state of this embryo crystal must therefore be represented by a combination of many such vectors— corresponding to a superposition of a wide variety of different orientations of this handful of incoming atoms.

■ Life Forms and Living Systems

The key question now becomes, How, out of this initial ambiguity, this superposition of potential crystals, is it possible for a definite, fixed structure to evolve? It is not unreasonable to accept a quantum ambiguity when only two or three atoms are concerned, but what about ten atoms, one hundred, several million? Where does quantum ambiguity end and the well-defined properties of a real salt crystal begin?

A key theme within this book is that form and structure emerge spontaneously, for every system and every level in nature has its own authentic life. An immediate implication of this is that a previously ambiguous flux of forms is able to crystallize into something definite, which forms the basis for further growth. Indeed, in later chapters of this book the idea of crystallization will serve as a metaphor of the more general creation and manifestation of form within the universe. We will see how all systems, from atoms to galaxies, from crystals to bodies, from trees to human insights, are manifestations of spontaneous creation and coming into form.

Take, as a further example, a slime mold. This is an amoeba that lives on rotting vegetation found on the floor of woods and forests. An amoeba reproduces by simple division so that, given time, a single cell will spread out its progeny to cover a certain area. But such growth cannot continue unbounded; eventually, the food in the immediate region will be consumed, and the colony of individuals will face starvation. But at this point something remarkable occurs: The individual cells begin to move inward. First, they congregate, then group together to create a single, complex organism.

As the context of their life changes, a large number of individual, unconnected cells come together and sacrifice their individuality to form a single, sluglike organism in which each cell now plays a special role in the service of the whole. This collective slug now begins to move across the forest floor in search of a new area of nourishment.

Eventually, it stops and transforms yet again. This time it erects a thin stalk into the air, on the top of which grows a spore cap. From this cap burst a multitude of slime mold spores that drift across the forest floor and settle on fresh vegetation. From each spore develops a new amoeba and, by subsequent division, a new slime mold colony. The amoeba is therefore capable, depending on the context, of being both an individual and one cell in an organism. Cells can exist as an uncoordinated mass of individuals or can "crystallize" into a single, cooperative form. Clearly, within each individual is enfolded the potential of the collective. Yet the existence of collective is predicated on the individual.

This is but one example of how structure emerges out of the seemingly contingent behavior of a collection of individuals. In human society, a crowd of people can spontaneously form into a purposeful group. Indeed, a person is at one and the same time both a free individual and a member of a family, group, or political party. In turn, groups can become welded together as part of a nation. The whole meaning, value, and structure of the nation is enfolded within the lives of each individual, and, likewise, the nation itself emerges out of the activities, beliefs, and actions of each individual.

An Indigenous group of people, for example, is far more than a collection of separate individuals, for it has its own unique authenticity that flows from its meaning, map, ceremony, and history. In this sense, the group is complete in itself and requires no authorization from anything outside itself. The group, as with everything else in nature, is inexhaustible in its richness, and while it may be possible to analyze its governance, structure, activities, and the like, according to some sociological theory, and even to gain a measure of insight through this, such an analysis will never exhaust the meaning of the group.

In such a cohesive group, each individual is unique and sovereign. Each individual has a life, relationships, memories, hopes, and desires. Each individual has skills and a role to play, and each individual has a responsibility to assist in the group's ceremonies and activities. Just as the group is authentic in itself, so is the individual. Both are inexhaustible, and neither can be reduced to the other. Yet each, in a sense, is enfolded within the other.

That a group contains individuals is perfectly clear, but it does not follow from this that the group is composed of individuals like a car is composed of parts. For it is also the case that each individual, in a sense, unfolds out of the group in that, to a great extent, the values and position that an individual holds flow out of the group. For example, the way a person perceives and interacts with the world is to some extent conditioned by the language he or she speaks. But language is clearly a societal activity. Just as a quantum system must be treated as an indivisible whole, so, too, each time we speak, the meaning cannot be exclusively ascribed to a single individual but is in a sense nonlocal and distributed over the whole of society. So while within the group can be found the individual, so, too, within the individual can be found the group.

But suppose that the structures of the natural world are also of this nature, rather than simply being collections of smaller components such as molecules, atoms, and elementary particles. In such a case, it makes sense to talk about the whole world as being alive. The growth of a city, a crystal, or a human embryo; the flow of a river; and rush-hour traffic would all have something in common. Systems unfold into the world with their own cohesive structures, forms, and laws.

▇ Candles, Crystals, and Superconductors

The prevailing overview of physics has conditioned us to think in terms of large-scale structures as being constructed of smaller and therefore simpler elements. This approach, involving the search for a most ultimate elementary particle, was questioned in the last chapter, and now it is possible to find examples in which smaller and "more elementary" levels need not necessarily be simpler and more fundamental. The motivations and beliefs of individuals in a crowd, for example, may be vastly more complicated than those of the crowd itself. Indeed, if one attempts to break down a crowd and analyze individuals, in an effort to explain some sort of group behavior, rather than arriving at a more simple ground, one would encounter a wide variety of conflicting opinions and standards of behavior.

In terms of the phase space picture, it may require an astronomical number of dimensions to describe the physical background out of which a natural structure emerges. Remember that for each particle in a many-particle system, six dimensions are required. But when a large number of material or human individuals are together, they may form a group with a pattern of what could be called collective behavior, which requires a smaller number of variables.

Slime molds and human societies are examples of collective ordering in living systems. In some cases, the larger form is more complex than the simpler elements; in others, the reverse is true. But in every case, the collective form creates its own appropriate level of description and behavior that is not exclusively reducible to any level below.

The same thing is seen in the inanimate world of plasmas, superconductors, and superfluids. The vortex in a river, for example, is a persisting form that survives out of the very activity of the flowing water. Its stability is the direct result of the constant movement of the river; if this flow should be reduced, the vortex would die. A fountain in the square of a Renaissance city is another dynamic pattern that is maintained by the constant circulation of water.

Even a candle flame represents stability within flux. The flame is a living, dynamic process. It lives on the edge of constant extinction. The flame persists, however, because oxygen from the air is constantly reaching it and diffusing across its boundary in order to feed the chemical reactions of burning within. Likewise, the heat of the flame is constantly melting the candle, and this molten wax is constantly diffusing up the wick, evaporating, and being carried up into the flame as fuel. Each aspect of the flame is ephemeral, yet taken together they produce a flame that can burn throughout the night. So the candle flame has its origin in constant flux, and in a sense, that flame is alive.

Physics tells us that a rock is composed of a vast number of atoms. And these same atoms, which at the quantum level of description are enfolded in ambiguity, conspire to engage in a great dance whose collective manifestation is a rock. The rock is pure dance. Its very rockness, its inertness, its whole inner voice, are the manifestation of this constant movement and flux.

To take a more specific example, some of the electrons in a metal are free to move around within the stable lattice of atoms. Indeed, a vast number, around a septillion (the number one followed by twenty-four zeroes) of them, move so freely that they behave just like a gas. Physics teaches that an electric current is nothing more than a gas of electrons that drifts through a metal wire from one end to the other. Since each electron is negatively charged, the drifting of the gas produces a flow of electrical charge along the wire—in other words, an electric current. The overall effect is similar to the flow of traffic on a highway.

But unlike automobiles, electrons are constantly bumping into each other as well as colliding and scattering off obstacles in their path. The net result of all these collisions is to retard the drift of electrical charges—which then manifests itself as an electrical resistance. The effect of electrons constantly bumping into atoms in the lattice is to give these atoms a series of tiny kicks and so increase their vibrations. The faster the atoms vibrate, the more energy is stored within the lattice and the warmer the metal feels. In other words, the act of passing an electric current through a metal causes it to heat up. An electric light bulb glows white hot because a large number of electron collisions with obstacles heats the wire to incandescence.

The drifting electrons in a metal are like an unruly crowd of fans that jostle each other as they rush for the exits after a ball game. But suppose that a new and delicate interaction is introduced into the system, one that tends to operate in an attractive way between pairs of electrons. Although, on an individual basis, the energy inherent in any particular collision vastly exceeds the immediate influence of this new interaction, something startling happens when the temperature of the metal is lowered below a certain critical level. As the temperature drops, so, too, do the average speed and energy of the electrons until, at some critical point, the electron gas stops acting like a jostling crowd and begins to behave as a single, collective entity. Now the gas as a whole engages in a sort of dance in which every electron has a part to play. The result is called a *superconducting state*, one in which the whole gas of electrons moves through the metal lattice without any scattering or electrical resistance.

The state of every quantum system is described by a wave function, and in the case of the superconductor, it turns out that it is the overall *form* of this wave function that is vital. Indeed, this form choreographs the dance of an astronomical number of electrons over a large distance. But the form itself does not lie in any one electron, nor is it a collection of individual contributions. Rather, the form is a direct manifestation of the system as a whole.

Each level of nature has its own authenticity and life. In this case, it lies in the collective behavior of the entire electron gas, a coordinated dance of a septillion electrons. And as this collective dance moves through the metal, all resistance vanishes, and it becomes a superconductor. Suppose that a single electron within this flow approaches an obstacle. As an individual particle in interaction with others, its natural inclination would be to scatter, that is, to hit the obstacle and fly backwards and, in the process, collide with other electrons and so create a tiny local region of turbulence within the overall current flow. Add together all these turbulences, and a much larger resistance to flow is established. But in a superconductor, each electron has become the particular expression of a great dance and is subject to the active form of the whole. While the new attractive interaction between any two electrons (such interactions become important in superconducting ceramics at some one hundred degrees below room temperature or in other metals at much lower temperatures) is incredibly small, when taken as a whole the dance of electrons conspires to guide each individual electron around obstacles without scattering. Individuals have sacrificed their freedom in order to engage in a greater movement. A new, stable, dynamic order has emerged out of a background of flux. And this means that the whole gas can be characterized by just a few variables that describe its overall flow, rather than in terms of the individual motions of an astronomical number of electrons.

Something similar happens in liquid helium when it is cooled very close to absolute zero. At this point, the liquid becomes what is called a superfluid, a liquid that is able to flow without any resistance or viscosity. Again, the form of the whole, the wave function, determines the motion of each individual atom within the liquid and thereby guides it past obstacles without collisions. In both cases, it is the overall form of the wave function that governs individual behavior. Moreover, this form acts to resist tiny fluctuations and random collisions.

Superconductivity is a quantum effect, yet the spatial extension of the wave function that describes the flowing electron gas in a superconductor extends along the wire itself and may end up being several centimeters in length. This really comes as a considerable surprise, for we tend to think of quantum theory as applying only at the level of the incredibly small—to molecules, atoms, elementary particles, and other entities that are far beyond our perceptual experience. But a superconducting wire can be picked up in the hand—or at least it could if we did not mind the extremely low temperatures involved—yet this superconductor is a single quantum entity described by a single quantum mechanical wave function.

In fact, superconductivity and superfluidity are not the only cases of quantum systems that manifest themselves at our own scale. The human nervous system behaves in many ways like a quantum device, for it is capable of responding to just a few molecules of a strong-smelling substance or to a few photons of light. Indeed, some physicists and neuroscientists have speculated that human consciousness itself is the direct manifestation of a holistic quantum system. Consciousness acts as a whole: Its manifestations are global and extend across the whole brain, and certain of its properties hint at some sort of global quantum process.

Of course, to suggest that mind is nothing but a wave function would be not only an oversimplification but also a trivialization. Yet the hypothetical quantum nature of the brain may hold some clues to its operation. Think, for example, of what happens when we look up into the night sky and contemplate the very faintest star. Our brains are actually responding to something that occurs at the quantum level. They are part of a direct quantum link between our nervous system and a quantum event within a star, something that happened far out in the galaxy and long ago in time. In turn, this quantum connection between the retina of the eye (which is an extension of the brain) and the star unfolds within the brain itself and gives rise to all our mental reflections and feelings about the vastness of time and space.

▇ Plasmas and Crowds

An even more interesting example of large-scale quantum behavior comes from what are called *plasma vibrations* in a metal. As we saw earlier, electrons in a metal at room temperature normally behave like individuals in a crowd who are involved in all sorts of random movements and collisions. The form of wave function in such cases is not all of a piece (or coherent, as physicists call it), and unlike the case of the superconductor, it does not represent a global dance that extends across the whole metal. In the normal case, two electrons that are colliding at one end of the metal have very little to do with the way some other electron is moving at the other end. As a result, the total wave function looks as if it were made up of a large number of individual, local contributions that are not coordinated together in any way. The wave function does not show any significant overall global form, nor is it correlated over long periods of time. As a result, at room temperature, quantum effects are always localized, and because individual effects tend to average out, it is not possible to have a global quantum effect that extends to macroscopic distances.

So, on the one hand, some quantum systems are nothing more than crowds of individuals, but, on the other, there are the vast, correlated ballet dances of the superconductor or superfluid. It is also possible to have systems in which both global and individual behaviors are enfolded within one system. Look, for example, at what happens when a little extra energy is supplied to the gas of freely moving electrons in a metal. Normally, a small increase in energy simply causes the electrons to move that much faster and to engage in even more collisions. As a result, the wave function becomes even less coherent than it was before. But if energy is supplied in a certain critical way, something dramatically different takes place. It is as if a musical instrument had been struck or a singer's voice had begun to resonate with a wine glass.

What happens is that the electron gas begins to move as a whole. It oscillates like a giant spring, and just as with a superconductor, all the electrons in the gas contribute to this new global dance. But their individual motions are not totally suppressed, for the dance is more complex—it is both local and nonlocal, both individual and collective. Enfolded within the apparently chance motions of each electron is the contribution it makes to the collective whole. If one were to look at just a few electrons in some local region of the metal, they would appear to be moving at random. It is only when we step back to observe the gas of electrons as a whole that this new, collective plasma wave is seen.

As with superconductivity and superfluidity, the quantum effect of the plasma wave extends across macroscopic distances.

The wave function for the electron gas must now express the global dance of the plasma (the collective motion of the whole gas) as well as allow for the local individual motions of each electron. It therefore contains or enfolds a part that has a global quality (it consists of a few variables that express the collective behavior of the gas as a whole) and another that is purely local and involves the uncoordinated combination of very many small, individual, local contributions.

The plasma vibration in a metal is more subtle and complicated than is the superconducting state, for a new level of description is involved in which the electrons in a metal behave partly as individuals yet, at the same time, contribute to a large-scale coherent oscillation. The wave function for the plasma was originally discovered by David Bohm, who said that, at the time, he had the sense that the plasma was alive. And its rich layers of behavior do indeed have far more to do with what we know about life than with the motions of a machine.

If these were the only examples of the emergence of order, structure, and coherence in the quantum world, they would simply be scientific curiosities. But such behavior is really much closer to being the rule than the exception. Think of the DNA molecule present in every one of the cells in your body. This molecule is able to interact quantum mechanically with other much smaller molecules and in this way coordinate the metabolic activity of the cell. Under the influence of other quantum mechanical processes, DNA is also able to unfold and unwind itself, then wind back again into the familiar double helix. Clearly, we are dealing with a quantum object.

Cats and Color

This act of unwinding and unfolding is somewhat of a puzzle, for it seems to be guided by an overall global principle. If you try to explain the way in which a DNA unfolds in terms of local quantum events and interactions, the whole process would take far too long and life as we know it would not be possible. At one and the same time, DNA is therefore a quantum object and a manifestation of global properties.

Quantum theory, we saw, deals in ambiguity, for quantum states are represented by the combination of all possible vectors in Hilbert space. Schrödinger's cat, we are told, is a combination of live and dead cats. But one's own eyes are not combinations of blue, brown, and green. One's hair is not simultaneously short, long, black, red, curly, and straight. While I do not believe that DNA and the genetic code constitute the final answer to the questions of life and evolution, it is certainly true that to a great extent the forms of our bodies are enfolded within the genetic code carried by the DNA molecule. And this structure was, in turn, the product of DNA molecules held in the germ cells of our parents and their parents and their parents, and so on, back into the mists of evolution.

On the one hand, we have a quantum system, a DNA molecule, and on the other, a form that must be stable and well defined over decades and indeed, through inheritance, over thousands and millions of years. How is quantum theory to explain this? How are stability and definiteness to be contained within indeterminacy and ambiguity? Clearly, the conventional Hilbert space picture introduced in the previous chapter requires radical revision in order to take into account the emergence of global forms out of ambiguity and chance. In the sections that follow, I am going to propose a way of modifying and extending quantum theory.

■ Hilbert Space Revisited

In conventional quantum theory, the state of a system is represented by a vector that points in a given direction. But the properties of Hilbert space allow for all possible combinations of vectors to stand as equally legitimate descriptions. It suggests that different vectors, representing different states of the system, can all be superposed together. In the case of Schrödinger's cat paradox, this leads to a totally absurd conclusion, for a combination of a live and a dead cat is a legitimate outcome in conventional quantum theory.

But a superconductor can be held in the hand, and at this level its quantum mechanical wave function must therefore be well defined and extend over macroscopic dimensions. A superconducting current may be used to power the electromagnet of an MRI scanner in a hospital or the levitation equipment in a Japanese MagLev train. There can be no ambiguity about its existence; the superconducting state is a definite fact within our large-scale world and demands an equally definite quantum description.

While the normal state of electrons in a metal can be represented by a product of many different local contributions, the state of a superconductor cannot. There must be a single, well-defined wave function whose form corresponds to the coherent movement of all the electrons in the gas and extends for many centimeters. But this seems to suggest that vectors in Hilbert space can no longer be combined in a totally arbitrary way, for then the system would be described by a superposition of different possibilities.

In its conventional formulation, all possible combinations of Hilbert space vectors are legitimate descriptions of a quantum system. This implies that even macroscopic states can be combined together to produce ambiguous possibilities, as is the case with Schrödinger's cat. Yet the flow of current in a superconductor is not an ambiguous phenomenon. How, then, can this apparent dilemma be resolved? How is it possible to move from a description in which all possible combinations of vectors are permitted to one involving the defined variables needed to describe the behavior of a coherent system? The only conclusion is that the whole nature of Hilbert space must be radically changed. In this chapter I want to suggest that somehow natural systems must spontaneously develop their own unambiguous structures and collective order. Such systems create their own levels of description, their own internal maps.[1]

Just as the crowd, slime mold, superconductor, superfluid, and plasma develop their own coherent order, so, too, Hilbert space must acquire a structure that mirrors the internal structure of collective and cooperative systems. To give a pictorial image, Hilbert space develops a rich inner structure of subspaces and of subspaces within subspaces. Hilbert space becomes a Chinese box, or rather something even more elaborate, for each box contains a number of compartments that hold boxes containing their own compartments. It is this Hilbert space structure that reflects the new cooperative structure of the quantum system with its global form.

Yet within the structured Hilbert space, each of its subspaces is complete unto itself and contains anything from two to an infinite number of dimensions. Indeed, it is possible to describe a quantum system completely in terms of vectors inside this subspace. In fact, cooperative quantum systems will now have a sort of two-level description. At one level, there is an ambiguous combination of vectors within a specific subspace. But added to this is the information on the way that particular subspace is nested within the rich structure of subspaces and of subspaces within subspaces. While the first level of the description refers to quantum fluctuations and ambiguities within the system, the second level refers to its overall well-defined global form (Figure 4.1).

▓ Quantum Bureaucracy

An image of what is being proposed in this chapter is given by comparing conventional Hilbert space with a giant warehouse and the new, richly structured Hilbert space with an office complex. In the phase space approach, a system is defined as being

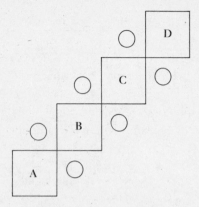

Figure 4.1.   A pictorial metaphor of a structured Hilbert space. The subspaces A, B, C . . . all contain vectors while the space around them is empty. The state of a quantum system, a Hilbert space vector, can lie in only one of these subspaces and can never contain components from some other region of Hilbert space.

at a precise location within a warehouse. In conventional quantum theory, the system is in all possible combinations of different somewheres. But the new structured Hilbert space description demands that the system be inside some definite office—for example, it is in the east block, on the tenth floor; turn left at the elevator; it is in the fifth room on the right. The set of directions that enables us to locate a particular office within the complex corresponds to the well-defined, physical, and dynamic structure of the quantum system. But once we are within that office, the old quantum ambiguity remains, for the system is described in terms of all possible combinations of vectors within that particular subspace.

From the perspective of someone living inside a subspace, things look just as they do in the orthodox interpretation. A quantum system is described by all possible combinations of vectors within the subspace, and to this extent, it still involves ambiguity. But other aspects of ambiguity are resolved by the fact that we now know that these vectors must lie in one specific subspace rather than some other. Moreover, vectors from one office room cannot combine with those from another.

This gives a new definiteness to the description, for while the combination of vectors within a subspace may still be arbitrary, they have been narrowed down to a particular region—a subspace—within Hilbert space. And what makes this so exciting is that this narrowing down, this crystallization of an actuality out of many possibilities, corresponds directly to the way in which coherence naturally emerges within a quantum system.

From now on, I want to suggest, while there may be ambiguity *within* a subspace, at least we know that a coherent quantum system lies in one subspace and not another. This partial resolution of quantum ambiguity corresponds to the fact that the quantum system now has an overall global form. It tells us something new about the overall structure or order of the system. So this novel approach to quantum theory takes into account the way systems can spontaneously evolve their own structure and form.

As we saw earlier, when a superconductor, superfluid, or plasma structures itself, it also develops a new description that reflects its internal coherence. This new description involves a set of collective coordinates—unambiguous parameters that describe its large-scale structure. In turn, these parameters govern the overall large-scale form of the wave function. It is this form, for example, that can act to direct individual electrons to take part in the global dance of a superconductor. The connection with the new idea of a structured Hilbert space becomes clear, for knowing in which particular subspace the system's vectors are located is equivalent to knowing about these collective parameters.

It may now even be possible to find a bridge between, on the one hand, quantum theory and, on the other, phase space. While Heisenberg's uncertainty principle negates the whole idea of trajectories and points in phase space, the idea that a system is associated with a particular region of a highly structured Hilbert space corresponds to the notion that the system could be within a general region of phase space. The correspondence is not exact, but it suggests that rather than points and trajectories, one may at least be able to deal with regions of phase space and their mutual transformations and interconnections. Indeed, at some point, it may be possible to develop a formalism that brings the two approaches even closer.

■ Penrose Tiles and Quasi Crystals

This novel proposal that quantum structures can spontaneously evolve out of a sea of uncertainty can be illustrated by returning to our example of the growth of a crystal. Just as a crystal emerges out of a concentrated solution, so, too, does a rich Hilbert space crystallize out of underlying quantum ambiguity.

The crystal begins its life in an ambiguous fashion when a few atoms orient themselves as they enter their mutual spheres of attraction. At this stage, the crystal is represented by all possible combinations of vectors in a structureless Hilbert space. The embryo crystal is an ambiguous superposition of very many different states, each one representing a different orientation of just a handful of atoms. Yet the final outcome, after growth is completed, is a large-scale crystal whose existence is quite definitely unambiguous; therefore, its description requires a location within a highly structured Hilbert space.

The idea is that, at an appropriate scale of complexity, quantum systems will begin to structure themselves under the influence of their mutual interactions. In this way, a collective form begins to emerge, which then acts back on the system to stabilize it and maintain its structure. This new level is complete in itself, and the global form of its wave function, or the rich structure of its Hilbert space, acts to choreograph all its components.

This is not a case of a more complex system being created out of an aggregation of components, as is the case with a machine, but of a truly holistic process whose meaning lies in the operation of the whole system. Yet again we see how form and pattern emerge in a collective way out of the system as a whole.

This phenomenon can be seen even in the case of crystal growth. Conventional theory indicates that the final position of each atom in the crystal is determined by purely local forces, that is, by the electrical repulsions and attractions between neighboring atoms. An incoming atom approaches the growing crystal in a blind way. It moves around, adjusting its position and orientation until its energy is minimized and it feels most stable. In this fashion, it is generally assumed, the crystal grows in a relatively mechanical way by accumulating more and more atoms. But the problem with this account is that there now exist curious new materials called *quasi crystals* that seem to defy this process of growth.

Quasi crystals are connected with some curious theoretical ideas of the mathematician and physicist Roger Penrose and suggest that the growth of all crystals—and indeed the behavior of very many quantum processes—is governed by forms and structures that have a global nature. As I have already suggested quantum systems are by their very nature wholes and give rise to all manner of holistic structures such as crystals, superconductors, superfluids, plasma, and possibly even certain large-scale structures in the human brain. Holistic structures are profoundly different from mechanical structures that are constructed of individual parts. An atom is more than a collection of elementary particles. A human being is more than a mass of cells. Each level in nature has its own authenticity and law of being.

But what has this to do with the growth of a crystal? Scientists have noticed that a wide variety of natural and artificial structures, from crystals to the tiles on a kitchen floor, can be built by fitting together simple, repeating shapes. An endless number of pyramids or cubes can be fitted together to produce an ever-expanding structure. Likewise, triangular, square, and even hexagonal tiles can be used to cover a kitchen floor. But what seemed to be missing in nature were pentagonal tiles—objects with a five-fold symmetry. By playing around with general five-sided objects, mathematicians soon learned that it is impossible to lay them side by side in such a way that they can spread out indefinitely and cover an unlimited area. The problem is that in laying down five-sided tiles one soon runs into problems. Fitting each tile to its neighbors in a blind way eventually pro-

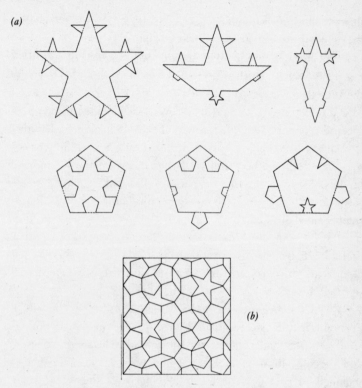

Figure 4.2.   In general, a set of five-sided tiles will not cover a floor without eventually overlapping or creating a gap. But these curiously shaped tiles are capable of covering a plane of infinite extent.

duces a gap, or a tile jam, at which point the whole process comes to a halt. This was the explanation offered as to why such structures were missing in nature: They simply could not grow without getting stuck at some point.

But then Roger Penrose, and some other mathematicians, showed that it was possible to design special sets of five-sided tiles that could be laid side to side so as to cover an endless surface without ever jamming or leaving gaps. The striking thing about these new shapes is that the actual process of tile laying has to be done in a special way. It is no good thinking about five-sided shapes and how they could be arranged at the purely local level, that is, by cutting out some five-sided shapes and simply moving them around until they fit together, without taking into account the growing pattern across the floor (Figure 4.2).

In the case of triangular, square, or hexagonal tiles, it does not really matter which side is fitted to which. Provided one cuts the tiles all the same size, one side of a tile can always be turned to expose another side, and whichever sides happen to be glued together does not affect the growth of the whole pattern. But this is not the case with Penrose's pentagonal tiles, for while two tiles may be fitted together in more than one way, if the wrong side is chosen, eventually a tile jam or a gap will occur. It is not possible to decide precisely how to lay these tiles simply by looking at their immediate neighbors. Instead, the person laying the tiles must know something about the overall evolving pattern so that each tile can be located according to a global plan. In other words, a particular tile's role within the evolving pattern is determined by the whole.

Does this begin to seem familiar? It sounds as if the nature of the individual is determined by the *form* of the whole. This is similar to what happens with the slime mold, the superconductor, and the superfluid. It evokes the idea of a quantum system in which each part is governed by the form of the whole wave function and systems that cannot be reduced to the simple interactions of parts.

But back to those five-sided figures: Up to now, we have been talking about tiles cut from a piece of cardboard or plastic. But is there also a connection between Penrose's five-sided shapes and a real quantum system? In 1984, an Israeli physicist, Dany Schectman, discovered that an alloy of aluminum and manganese could be grown into a quasi crystal that exhibits the same "unnatural" fivefold symmetry. Since that first announcement, the existence of quasi crystals has been well established.

Such objects appear to defy the conventional idea that crystals grow by purely local process, for example, the adjustment of each incoming atom to fit alongside its neighbors. For a real quasi crystal to grow, it must have some idea of the whole pattern into which it is to fit.

Conventional quantum theory teaches that the growth of a crystal is driven purely by local considerations of energy, with each atom blindly maneuvering into a comfortable position next to its neighbors in such a way that its energy is minimized. But there will always be an inherent ambiguity in its final position because the atom could be turned around and still fit within its neighbors. This cannot be the case with a quasi crystal. The position of each atom in a quasi crystal must somehow reflect the restrictions of the global form demanded by the crystal as a whole. It is as if additional information about the global form of the whole crystal determines the final orientation of each incoming atom, which seems to suggest that a global wave function acts to steer each atom toward its correct location as it approaches the crystal.[2] Such ideas may seem bizarre to conventional physicists, but they are entirely in keeping with the sorts of ideas being explored in this chapter.

In terms of the new ideas being explored in this book, the first stages of growth are represented by a superposition of vectors in a general Hilbert space. However, as the embryo crystal reaches a certain size, Hilbert space itself begins to crystallize into a definite structure, and from now on, the vector corresponding to the growing crystal will be confined to a particular subspace. Although all possible combinations of vectors are still permitted within that subspace, the wave function now possesses an overall global form. Other subspaces may correspond to different possible global forms of a crystal but not to the one possessed by the actual crystal in question and are therefore ruled out by the actuality of our particular crystal.

It is this structured Hilbert space that determines an associated global wave function that acts to guide the continuing growth of the crystal. From now on, incoming atoms will be guided by the global pattern of the quasi crystal and will bond together according to a larger design. It is possible that not only the crystal itself but the region of space-time associated with the space of the crystal is also "crystallized out." There may be no absolute separation between material structures and space-time, for the appearance of one is always associated with the other. So, again, form and structure appear spontaneously within a quantum mechanical system.

■ The Collapse of Ambiguity

It so turns out that Penrose himself has made a strikingly similar speculation. The first few atoms that congregate together are, he suggests, in an ambiguous state so that the crystal as a whole is represented by a combination of different states, that is, by a superposition of wave functions. Then, at some critical point, this superposed wave function "collapses" into a definite form, and from then on, the crystal will develop according to a particular global pattern.

Penrose's radical idea is that the collapse from ambiguity to a definite global form is brought about by the nature of space-time itself. In his general theory of relativity, Einstein had proposed that the presence of matter, or energy, acts to give a curvature to space-time. Penrose, in turn, suggests that at a particular point in its growth the embryo crystal reaches such a size that it creates a tiny region of curved space-time around itself. At first, many such different curved space-times will exist, each of microscopic dimensions and the whole being superposed together. But at some point, space-time grows to such a size that a single quantum of gravity—called a *graviton*—is created. In Penrose's opinion, there is now no going back after this region of space-time has been created. In fact, he suggests that this causes the collapse of the wave function from ambiguity into something definite. At this point, one single global form crystallizes out of the initial ambiguity of the growing quasi crystal.

The graviton or a quantum of space-time is essentially non-local and cannot exist, so Penrose believes, in an ambiguous state. So a collapse from ambiguity must always occur when a crystal, or any other structure, reaches a certain critical size, one large enough to be associated with a fixed region of space-time. From this point on, no superposition of wave functions is permitted, and only a single global wave function exists, which then has the effect of guiding the continuing growth of the crystal.

■ Crystallization of Form

But I want to suggest that collective quantum structures go even further than this. Indeed, the mechanism of growth associated with Penrose's quasi crystal, this evolution of a structured Hilbert space, is not an isolated curiosity of the natural world involving fivefold symmetries. Rather, it is true of all crystals and of all coherent forms. At first, the form of a crystal, the molecule in a living cell, or some other structure is ambiguous. The first few atoms that happen to come together have no well-defined order and are represented by all possible combinations of vectors in a structureless Hilbert space. But as the crystal grows, a definite and coherent structure emerges. Atom upon atom fits into an expanding lattice whose structure eventually reaches macroscopic dimensions. This lattice is the backbone of the crystal and there can be no ambiguity about its repeating structure. Moreover, it is described by a wave function with a global form and associated with a particular Hilbert subspace. It is this overall form that guides the future growth of the crystal.

Physicists normally believe that the electrical forces between atoms are sufficient to cause each incoming atom to fit into the developing crystal structure. Why should any other process be needed to account for crystal growth? Remember the case of the superconductor. There, the ordinary electrical repulsions between electrons at first appear to dominate the behavior of a normal electron gas. They are certainly far larger than the tiny additional attraction that superconductivity demands. But, as it turns out, it is this much smaller attraction that ends up orchestrating the whole gas. Owing to this tiny attraction, it is possible for an astronomical number of electrons to engage in their collective dance, a dance that corresponds to a global wave function and that compels each individual electron to join in the collective motion of the whole.

In fact, it is not the strength of the interaction that matters but its very special form. (Technically speaking, the interaction links together those electrons in a superconductor that happen to have equal but opposite momentum.) Likewise, in a crystal, local electrical forces involving the attractions and repulsions of individual atoms may be quite strong and will be responsible for grossly moving atoms around. Nevertheless, the new ideas of this chapter suggest that the more subtle guiding activity of the global wave function itself comes to dominate the overall structure of the final crystal. Or to put it another way, it is the cooperative effect of the whole system that acts to direct its inner parts.

Something similar happens to all structures that grow to a macroscopic scale, from crystals, metals, and plastics to large biological molecules and even living cells. All must be similarly represented by vectors located in a subspace of a highly structured Hilbert space, and their growth can be subtly influenced by global considerations. Nature's systems are not simply collections of parts but are collective forms that are complete in themselves.

■ Schrödinger's Cat Revived

In one sense it is a small jump from a crystal to the paradox of Schrödinger's cat. A cat is a globally coordinated system. It has a complex overall form that contains organs composed of cells, each of which has a very definite structure and is involved in complex metabolic processes. Clearly, a live cat has a profoundly different order from a dead cat. A live and a dead cat refer to different subspaces of a structured Hilbert space. This difference goes beyond the example of the crystal given above, for clearly the live and dead cat refer to wholly different orders of structuring of a Hilbert space. There is no possibility of quantum ambiguity, no chance of the vectors from live and dead cats being combined together.

The resolution of the Schrödinger cat paradox is not unlike what happens during the growth of a crystal. The actual quantum process that triggers the Schrödinger cat event—the disintegration of a radioactive nucleus—may at first be ambiguous and represented by a mixture of all different possibilities. But, in turn, this disintegrating nucleus is coupled to an electronic apparatus, such as a Geiger counter, which amplifies the effects of a nuclear disintegration. The Geiger counter is connected to an electronic apparatus whose output triggers a mechanical device designed to smash a vessel containing cyanide. The initially ambiguous state experiences a series of electrical and mechanical amplifications as it progressively couples to larger- and larger-scale apparatuses, and in the process, this description crystallizes into one involving a highly structured Hilbert space. Within that Hilbert space, the combination of vectors representing the final outcome is located either in a region corresponding to a dead cat or within a profoundly different region corresponding to the various possible orientations of a live cat. (The different states, movements, and orientations of a live cat would each correspond unambiguously to different regions of the "live cat" sector of Hilbert space.) While there may be some ambiguity as to the fine details of the quantum state of the system, at the level of human observation there is no possible arbitrary quality—the cat is either alive or it is dead.

The idea that the forms and structures of nature can crystallize and exist through their collective nature can lead us to a radically different account of the universe than one based on a hierarchy of orders that emerge out of a single-most fundamental physical level.

CHAPTER
FIVE

THE SYMPHONY
OF LIFE

The fact that we can see the plasma, the superfluid, and the superconductor as physical manifestations of cooperation within nature helps us transcend the rigid distinction between living and nonliving entities. A new map of nature is therefore emerging, one in which the whole world is alive with meaning. In this chapter, we will move even deeper into this map and begin to see living nature as a complex and sensitive web of information in which cells, molecules, and minds enter into communication with each other and join the ever-changing dance of form and structure.

■ Coherence in Biological Systems

In 1968, theoretical physicist Herbert Fröhlich, who had earlier helped physicists to understand just what was happening in a superconductor, proposed that coherent vibrations of energy are the key feature of living systems. While these vibrations have a quantum mechanical origin, they can extend over regions of millimeters or even centimeters in length and, Fröhlich suggested, could well be the basis of all life.

Fröhlich and others have pointed out how large-scale oscillations of energy can be used to coordinate a system. In living systems, these oscillations may create highly sophisticated degrees of order within a cell and possibly even within the human brain. For, after all, living systems are distinguished from those that are dead by their very coherence, the way their various parts are able to interact in concert. A cell or an animal is able to preserve this essential functioning even when its environment changes.

Fröhlich contends that global oscillations of energy and coherences that stretch right across a cell are responsible for this coordinated activity. Life, it appears, is a direct manifestation of an idea that fits right into the present notion of a structured Hilbert space.

Currently, one of the pioneering ideas about the brain is that it is a coherent quantum system, an idea that goes straight back to Herbert Fröhlich. Indeed, some physicists are now pursuing the analogy between the brain and a superfluid or superconductor. Consciousness, they argue, is all of a piece; it is coherent and cannot be reduced to any classical mechanistic model. Just as the electrons in a superconductor engage in a global dance in which each individual movement is guided by the whole, so, too, individual activities of nerve cells may be coordinated into a much wider dance of thought. If this is correct, it would mean that the very structure of the brain has evolved to facilitate these coherent states.

Coherent oscillations should be capable of carrying, in an encoded fashion, an enormous amount of information, and the physical brain is dedicated to the production and interplay of the complex and subtle collective oscillations. Its structure allows for quantum processes to dance across macroscopic distances. In this sense, the brain and the highly structured Hilbert space are mirrors of each other.

Light and Life

The forms of nature are subtle and far ranging. When one moves from the lattice structure of a crystal or the dance of electrons in a superconductor to the coherent oscillations in the human brain, the distinction between animate and inanimate begins to blur. A particularly striking suggestion is that light itself may play a key role in living systems.

Light has a powerful mythical history in the creation of the world. In the Judeo-Christian religion, light was the result of the first act of creation, and in this sense, everything that exists comes from light. Light fills the entire universe, and there is not one region of space, however remote, that is not crisscrossed by complex patterns of electromagnetic radiation. Indeed, the random noise that can be picked up by a microwave dish facing an empty region of the sky is believed to be the actual radiation present at the Big Bang origin of the universe. The radiation that once filled the embryo universe is present everywhere; as space expanded over billions of years, so this aboriginal radiation was stretched out into longer and longer wavelengths until it forms the hiss that can be picked up by a microwave dish today.[1]

Even the smallest region of space is filled with radiation from the extremely low frequencies of the Big Bang remnants, through the range of radio waves, from visible light and into ultraviolet, and so up to gamma rays of the highest energy. This radiation comes from stars, from supernovas, from quasars, from the event horizon of black holes, and from the twisting magnetic fields that stretch across vast regions of empty space. Moreover, all this light is carrying information—it conveys information about its origin, in a nuclear process deep within the heart of a star or as matter hurtles into a black hole. Every volume of space is alive with electromagnetic radiation and therefore packed with an immense amount of data about the whole universe.

Light is a highly efficient way of encoding and transmitting information. Think of the tremendous number of telephone calls, television programs, and telecommunications channels that can be carried on a single beam of light along a fiber-optic link. This light stretches to the limits of all space, so that each tiny region of space contains an amount of information far exceeding the memory capacity of all the largest supercomputers put together.

Indeed, every time you look into the night sky, some of this information enters your eye and then unfolds within the brain to give a picture of the universe of stars and galaxies.

Light is information and communication. But what is truly remarkable is the recent highly controversial idea that light may play a central role in all biological systems.[2] Fritz-Albert Popp, an active researcher in this field at the Institute of Biophysical Cell Research in Kaiserslautern, Germany, is associated with the Centre for Frontier Studies at Temple University, Philadelphia. While his ideas are not accepted by all physicists, they are certainly striking in their implications.

For many decades, it had been speculated that electromagnetic fields are associated with living systems. But research in this field is extremely difficult to carry out, since for every good, well-documented experiment there are many others that cannot be duplicated. Nevertheless, a number of experimentalists have been looking at this proposed bioradiation and have suggested that photons, quantum particles of light, are emitted from the DNA molecule.

DNA is the key molecule in the nucleus of every cell, and now it seems that this same molecule may be giving off a very weak level of radiation—just a few photons at a time. Experimentalists who have investigated the nature of this radiation believe that it is coherent—just like laser light, only enormously weaker in its intensity. A biological molecule, DNA, seems to be acting like a laser and producing collective vibrations in an electromagnetic field.

If this finding is confirmed, the question must be raised as to why. Nature does not normally do things without a reason. Why should the central molecule of life be emitting a very weak form of laser light? What could be its purpose?

An immediate answer is communication. Admittedly, it is just a conjecture but one that scientists like Popp are willing to make. Suppose that DNA is using electromagnetic radiation, coherent light, to communicate inside the cell. Light can penetrate across the cell and is ideally suited for transmitting information.

Could it be that the cell uses a two-level communication system—slower-speed communication via conventional molecular processes that take place around the DNA molecule and a much-higher-speed communication within the whole cell using coherent light?

Scientists are also looking at coherent radiation from individual cells. The idea is that the entire organism may be swimming in a "living," vibrating electromagnetic field. It may turn out, for example, that coherent light is being used as a communication system throughout the whole plant or animal—between DNA and the cell, between cell and cell, and between organ and organ. The entire organism may be a complex flow of information in which each cell and organ is responding to a constant flux of electromagnetic messages.

A living being would be a complex communications system in which coherent light ties together all its activities of metabolism and change. Then the very coherence of light would be acting to preserve an even greater coherence: that of a living, changing organism. In this sense, light is active information. It is a global and active information that stretches across the cell—indeed, the whole organism—and coordinates its efforts.

Individual animals may even be able to communicate with each other using electromagnetic radiation, just as do cells in a body. Indeed, one may ask, Is information, in the form of the coherent dance of fields of light, the essence of all life and the way that complex living systems coordinate themselves?

At this point, some readers may feel uneasy, for the idea of a complex flux of electromagnetic radiation that controls the activities of an organism begins to sound like a "life force." The idea of such a field of information has echoes of an élan vital, of an aura of energy that surrounds the organism and indicates its state of health. But in fact this is just what several scientists are claiming—that the radiation given out by healthy cells is quite different from that given out by those that are sick or dying!

Could it be that health is an active flow of information within the body, whereas sickness is a breakdown in that flow, an impoverishment of information? The ever-changing flux of information carried within the electromagnetic fields and in the complex interlocking of a wide variety of chemical reactions must be so subtle that to an external observer its very complexity may appear chaotic. Indeed, it is very difficult to distinguish between chaos and a flux of ever-changing complexity. So when sickness occurs, the overall coherence of these complex and subtle fields of information will begin to break down until all that is left will be the various individual processes. This could explain why scientists have discovered that what appears to be chaotic behavior within the heart or brain is characteristic of health, whereas simple, regular heartbeats, for example, presage a heart attack.

■ An Ocean of Information

This idea that living systems are sustained by highly complex fields of cooperative information may characterize not only living organisms but entire ecosystems, societies, and indeed the whole planet. Life is always fluctuating and exploring, whereas simple oscillations are more characteristic of machines and dead matter. Simple stability spells death, whereas vitality lies in the ability to support a complex and subtle pattern of global fluctuations. An ever-flowing, ever-changing pattern of meaning becomes life itself, and the boundary between the animate and the inanimate begins to dissolve.

The whole field of electromagnetic bioinformation is controversial, but it is engendering some interesting research and raising a variety of significant questions. Is it possible, for example, for an organism to gather electromagnetic information about the environment and then feed it back into itself? If this is true, then an electromagnetic sense must be added to those others of sight, sound, touch, taste, and smell. There is already considerable evidence that many animals use electromagnetic sensors to help them navigate.

The surface of the earth is alive with electromagnetic signals.

In addition to the magnetic field of the earth, radiation from the sun falls on the earth and its upper atmosphere. There are slow oscillations in which the electromagnetic field of the whole earth vibrates at a frequency of between seven and eight times every second. There are also waves of this activity high in the ionosphere and magnetosphere whose effects are ultimately felt on the surface of the earth. Indeed, the whole earth is a vast and complex sea of radiation whose strength and pattern vary very subtly from place to place, for the information encoded in each location is affected by the chemical composition of nearby rocks, by minerals, by underground streams, and by surface water. This radiation pattern is also modulated by the daily fluctuations in the earth's weather.

So within any tiny portion of the earth's surface there is encoded a vast reservoir of electromagnetic information, concerning not only the global state of the earth but also the details about the particular local area. As a bird flies through the air, an animal moves across the surface of the earth, or a fish swims in the ocean, so it may be picking up and responding to a sea of electromagnetic information far more complex than that in any radar signal or radio broadcast. Moreover, the organism may even be picking up the faint electromagnetic signals and modulations given by its prey or other members of its pack. It is quite possible that some of this vast reservoir of information is decoded by the animal so that direct information about its surroundings is constantly being received.

But electromagnetic information is only one of several possibilities. A vast ocean of information is also carried through sound. For a small mammal, this sea of sounds paints a detailed picture of all the transient patterns of life and movement within the immediate environment. An animal responds not only through the ears to what is "heard" but possibly at the cellular level to high-frequency vibrations and to low frequencies that cause the whole organism to oscillate in sympathy. The animal is aware of the way its own sounds are reflected back and transformed by the environment. It constantly interprets the complex symphony of bird song, insect sound, and animal cry. When it comes to whales and dolphins, this matrix of vibrational information may extend throughout the ocean for several hundred miles. And add to all this a sea of smells that, to a dog, for example, produces a vivid impression of the world around. Every living being is immersed in a rich, subtle, and multilevel ocean of information.

▪ DNA: The Molecule That Listens

If DNA is responsible for sending coherent photons into the cell, is it also possible for this radiation to be modulated and bounced back from the environment where it is detected by the same molecule? Could it be that DNA can actually "listen" to the environment around it?

The DNA molecule is a vast repository of information; it contains the whole history of the cell's ancestors and evolution. This information is expressed by directing, in exactly the right time sequence, the synthesis of various proteins, which become involved in, depending on their nature, growth, regular metabolism, or repair. DNA is often pictured as the chairperson of the board, the active principle at the top of the hierarchy.

But there are difficulties associated with such a one-way flow of instructions. For how precisely is the correct information selected at just the right moment for its expression? If the cell turns out a particular protein too late or too soon, it will disrupt its whole metabolism. Moreover, only a very small percentage of all the information stored in DNA appears ever to be used. What is the function of the rest, those silent areas of DNA? Do they simply contain garbled messages and discarded information from far back in the cell's evolutionary history? Or could they have the potential to exercise a useful function?

Suppose that DNA could actually listen and respond to the world around it. Suppose that a cell operates in a democratic fashion so that DNA becomes a venerated elder statesperson rather than a dictator. DNA would be like a giant set of reference books on metabolism and the synthesis of various proteins. And as with a reference book, the actual information selected would depend on a wider context: on the whole cell and on the organism of which it is a part—even perhaps, on the external environment.

The electromagnetic dance within the cell carries the data on the ever-changing context of the world outside and could play a role in selecting specific information from DNA. In this way, the genetic code would then be part of a much greater language, the conversation of the whole organism, a conversation that even extends far out into the environment. The DNA molecule itself would be constantly informed about its wider surroundings, and in turn, certain of its "hidden information" could, for example, be made active. It is even possible that the whole cell could act in an intelligent way and cause modifications within its own DNA. In other words, a mutation of the organism would be the cooperative response to some overall change in the global context in which the cell lives, rather than a purely random and purposeless event. Evolution would become a cooperative process, the outcome of a constant dialogue between other life forms and their entire environment.

The idea that life is a complex dance of meaning and information leads to yet other speculations. One idea that at first sight appears absurd, yet has been seriously proposed, is that food may contain not only nutrients but also information! When a predator hunts its prey, so this theory goes, it is seeking not just a source of protein but a source of information. In consuming its prey, it is ingesting a complex structure of information. In this way, information is passed between species.

While this idea sounds pretty far out, it is not too distant from that held by many indigenous peoples who view food as nourishing the whole person and not just the physical body. To the hunters of North America, eating caribou and buffalo is "good medicine," and a person thrives by consuming their meat, for it does more than supply bodily energy. According to this view, food acts to feed a person at many levels, so that certain foods that happen to be high in protein could in other ways be "bad medicine." Likewise, a Chinese shaman will perform an act of divination using the bone of a sheep or goat. The animal eats only of pure grass and drinks of pure water, the shaman says; therefore, the "universal" will be strong within the bone so that it can hear and see.

Could it be that this "universal" of Chinese tradition is in fact active information and global meaning? Is the web of life, the dance of predator and prey, one great ballet of ever-changing information? And is evolution the intelligent and continued development of this symphony of meaning? Indeed, if the individual organism is viewed as the manifestation of coherence and information, then the whole history and pattern of life's unfolding on earth must be seen in the same way. Synchronicities now become just one more aspect of this greater dance of meaningful patterns.

By introducing information as a key player, we also see how the division between life and the inanimate has begun to dissolve. We realize that all coherent systems can never be fully reduced to interacting components, for they are responding to a collective dance, a dance that represents the essential authenticity of that particular level of being.

Bohm's Causal Interpretation

The idea of an activity that lies within an overall form, such as the form of the wave function, and of information that controls the dance of life, is clearly far reaching. Similar ideas of "active information" are also being explored by David Bohm in his causal interpretation of quantum theory.[3]

Bohm's approach to quantum theory is radically different from the other interpretations that have been presented in this book. To begin with, Bohm does not accept that the electron has a dual wave/particle nature, nor that quantum events are indeterministic. In Bohm's view, the electron is a material particle and has no wavelike aspect.

Like any other particle, the electron is pushed and pulled by natural forces. It can be repelled or attracted by a nearby electrical charge or caused to swerve in its path by a magnetic field. But in addition to being acted on by the conventional forces of nature, Bohm hypothesizes, the electron (or any other quantum particle) is also subject to a radically different sort of field, one that is essentially quantum mechanical in nature. This new *quantum potential*, as Bohm calls it, acts in a radically different way from any other force or field that has hitherto been proposed in physics. Indeed, the unique properties of the quantum potential, and the electron's response to it, are ultimately responsible for all the novel features of quantum theory.

Bohm contends that this quantum potential represents a totally new type of force in physics. While its effects may not normally be felt at our scale of things, at the subatomic world level, the quantum potential begins to dominate and produces all kinds of curious effects. To begin with, unlike other forces, the effect of the quantum potential does not depend on its size or intensity but only on its overall form.

In our everyday world, the bigger a force, the stronger its push or pull and therefore the more marked its effect. A large magnet, for example, is able to lift bigger pieces of iron than a smaller and weaker magnet, and its effects are felt further away. Not so with the quantum potential, where what matters is not its size but its overall form. Even a very weak quantum potential can have a dominating effect on distant quantum objects.

The effect of the quantum potential could be compared with someone's saying "Fire" in a crowded theater. Whether the person shouts out loud or simply whispers to his or her neighbors, the result is the same: One's immediate reaction is to get out of the theater and call the fire department. What is important is not the intensity of the sound but the information it carries (its form)—in this case, that the theater is on fire. Similarly, the quantum potential operates not by pushing or pulling an electron but by providing it with information about its environment and thereby guiding its motion.

Just as with an organism that is informed by its surrounding field of electromagnetic information, so, too, the quantum potential provides information about the surrounding quantum environment. In turn, the electron responds to this information and so modifies its motion. Bohm has compared the quantum potential with the radar signal that directs a large ship as it approaches a harbor. The energy of the radar signal does not actually move the ship through the water, but the information carried in the radar signal causes the ship to change direction by giving form to the movement produced by the much greater but unformed power of its engines. In this way, the complex information within a much weaker (radar) signal gives form to a much larger energy (the engines).

Bohm and his colleague Basil Hiley have applied their new causal interpretation, as they call it, to a variety of cases normally treated by conventional quantum theory. In all cases, the quantum potential approach is able to account exactly for the observed experimental results. As an example, think back to the puzzling double-slit experiment. The fact that a single electron or photon is able to interfere with itself or "pass through two slits at once" defies the logic of our everyday world. The conventional interpretation suggests an essential ambiguity in the motion of an electron that is accounted for by making a superposition of motions in which the photon or electron passes through different slits. No such ambiguity is present in the causal interpretation. Rather, the quantum particle moves deterministically along a definite path, the fine details of this motion being determined by the quantum potential.

This quantum potential carries information about the entire experimental situation, including the position of the two slits and whether they are open or blocked. Even though an electron may be quite far from one of the slits, the information about the total experimental situation is actively carried by the quantum potential. So while the electron passes through only one slit, it is nevertheless guided by a pool of information that includes knowledge about the second slit.

From that point on, the picture resorts back to the old phase space map. Given precise knowledge of the electron's position and momentum, its trajectory can be determined exactly. But each electron leaves the source with a small difference in velocity, and so it will take a slightly different path from its predecessor. Given enough events, the results look exactly the same as that produced by wave interference.

Figure 5.1 shows the various paths open to an electron faced with two slits. The electron is in the position of a car driver who approaches a slip road leading to a cloverleaf intersection. With the slightest movement of the steering wheel, the car can end up traveling along a different highway and heading in an entirely different direction. Since each electron enters the experimental region with a very tiny difference in speed, the actual path it takes will be unpredictable—although totally deterministic. At the end of the experiment, after many different electrons have been shot toward the slits, the familiar interference pattern will be reproduced. Yet in Bohm's causal interpretation, no physical interference of waves has occurred; the electron is always traveling along a single, deterministic path but in response to a complicated, global pool of information.

In Bohm's causal interpretation, the motion of the electron is not uncertain or ambiguous. Every time the electron moves, it does so in an exactly determined way and in response to all the information contained in the quantum potential. This has led Bohm to speak about information as being "active." Traditionally, we think of information as being something stored in a book or on the floppy disk of a computer, but the information in the quantum potential is constantly acting to influence the motion of the electron.

Although Bohm rejects the Hilbert space picture and returns to phase space with its deterministic trajectories, there is a definite link between his idea of the quantum potential and the new ideas presented in this book. In Bohm's approach, active information is used to guide the electron along its deterministic path. In a way, the whole structure of active information corresponds to the

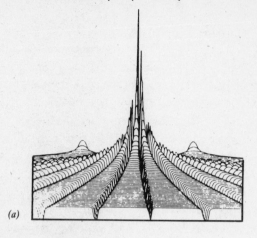

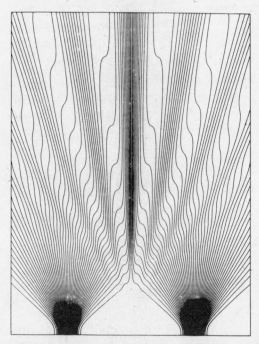

Figure 5.1. (*a*) The quantum potential for two slits as seen by an incoming electron. (*b*) The possible trajectories available to an electron after it has passed through one of the two slits. The action path taken depends upon the fine details of the electron motion as it passes through the slits. The slightest variation in its position will cause it to travel to a very different part of the screen. After many electrons have passed through the double slits, the result appears identical to that created by quantum interference.

complex structuring of Hilbert space, for the idea of this structured Hilbert space is that systems spontaneously form themselves into collective wholes and that the form of this whole acts to choreograph its various components and motions. In both cases, the form of the whole acts almost like a guiding intelligence and cannot be reduced to the effect of a collection of independent parts. Of course, Bohm's active information includes the whole environment of a quantum system. But this, too, can become a feature of structured Hilbert space, for as we shall see in the next section, the quantum system can enter into communication with other systems around it.

The superconductor, superfluid, plasma, slime mold, and crystal, together with coherent oscillations in living systems, could all be thought of as material (or energetic) manifestations of wholeness. Such systems are bound together in the same way that a human body is bound in health through the meaning of a person's life. And so the structures and activities of matter, mind, and life do not seem so far apart, and we no longer need to wonder why the structures of the universe of mind, matter, and life so often intersect or mirror each other.

▉ Communication and Change

The previous section dealt with the way in which nature's systems are immersed in a sea of active information about their whole inner and outer environment. It is possible to see how this would apply to a structured Hilbert space in which this structure can itself respond actively to an ever-changing environment and can enter into communication with it.

This idea of communication is really an investigation into the permeability and dissolution of the boundary a system creates in order to preserve its own autonomy. A human individual, for example, is sovereign over his or her body, mind, and experience. Yet individuals do communicate with each other; they share, relate, and at times, merge their horizons to form a new whole.

Love between two people dissolves all boundaries yet is based on mutual respect for each other's individuality. In a similar way, one can feel love for nature and a profound relationship with a tree or river, a relationship where a person merges with the inscape of the natural world.

In his autobiography *Memories, Dreams and Reflections,*[4] psychologist Carl Jung described how as a boy he spent long hours sitting and daydreaming on his favorite rock. At a certain point, the horizon between himself and the rock began to dissolve, and he was no longer certain who was rock and who was person, or who was thinking that thought. Jung's experience recalls a dream of the ancient Chinese philosopher Chuang Tzu who, when he awoke, could not recall if he were a butterfly dreaming he was Chuang Tzu or Chuang Tzu dreaming he was a butterfly.

If we are to appreciate fully the autonomy of levels and structures, we must also be able to understand how they relate and communicate together. But as soon as one begins to think about communication, one realizes that it has assumed a very special meaning in science, engineering, and linguistics. Ideas about communication have been greatly influenced by what is known to telecommunications engineers and computer experts as information theory. In the late 1930s, an MIT graduate student who was studying switches in circuits became interested in the way data are transmitted along telegraph lines and how some of them can be degraded by random electronic noise. The result was Claude Shannon's seminal paper "A Mathematical Theory of Communication," which stimulated a whole new area of science involving such things as information content, the rate at which information can be transmitted, random noise, and the idea of entropy. (Entropy was an idea first introduced in thermodynamics, the study of the relationship between heat and work, and is related to the degree of order and disorder in a system.)

Information or communications theory produced powerful results, and its insights were applied far outside their original field to the design of computers and artificial intelligence systems; communications networks; the operation of the human brain; linguistics; and the study of organizations, societies, and ecological systems.

But does information theory capture the essential spirit of what it really means to communicate and to enter into an understanding with someone else? Or does it only deal with a more limited conception? The problem with the theory is its essential passivity in the way it deals with how information is exchanged between a transmitter and a receiver. The transmitter generates a message, in code, which is then sent to the receiver, which decodes it and extracts the information. Communication is seen in terms of an exchange or interaction along a communication channel.

A similar idea prevails in some theories of linguistics in which communication is pictured like a cargo that is carried by a train between two cities. Language is the train and information the cargo. But this is a singularly passive picture of what it means to communicate with someone. To begin with, it makes a sharp distinction between the nature of the message and that of the transmitter or receiver. It also preserves an absolute distinction between the two people who are in communication. They merely exchange goods, in the form of language and gestures, which they then proceed to decode.

The French linguist G. Fauconnier has, to some extent, moved toward a more realistic theory of communication with his idea of "mental spaces."[5] Having a conversation, he proposes, is a creative business that cannot really be described in terms of the transmission of messages. Rather, each person is involved in a continuous act of creativity as he or she attempts to build "mental spaces" that will resonate, one with the other.

When you listen to someone else, you are in a state of constant activity, drawing on all your knowledge of past conversations and contexts. Some of what is said is ignored, but other parts seem replete with meaning. In this way, you begin to create a "mental space" of what the other person is talking about, a space that is richly furnished with meanings and allusions. While this space is partly built out of what you are hearing, a large part of it is actually created out of what you already know, what you have learned in your life, what you know about your own language, what you know about the other person and the particular context in which the conversation is taking place. As this mental space grows in the complexity of its structure, so, too, it acts to help you understand and integrate what is currently being said. For example, what at first appeared to be unimportant may now assume a greater value.

And so both parties in this conversation are constantly creating and furnishing their mental spaces, which then begin to resonate together and evolve. It is no longer possible to give any objective external account of the "information content" of the conversation because the value of the information is purely subjective and changes from moment to moment. It depends on the ever-changing context of the mental spaces themselves. What may be rich information to me may be of little value to you.

▚ The Dancing Brain

We can take this idea further by considering the brains, bodies, and nervous systems of two people engaged in conversation. The noted American neuroscientist Eric Kandel, who has spent a lifetime studying the fine details of nerve synapses in the sea slug, has made a particularly dramatic proposal. The very fine structure of our brains and the degree of sensitivity in delicate interconnections between the nerves are not fixed, he suggests, but can actually be changed by learning. This means that when new contexts come along, the structure of our brains can respond to them. Meaning can actually modify the structure of the human brain.

Kandel's ideas imply that during a conversation new meanings are constantly evolving, being modified, and resonating, one with the other. At the same time, the ultrafine structures of the two brains are changing. In fact, I would suggest, when the shared meaning between two people is very high, very delicate structures within their brains begin to mirror each other. At this physical level, the boundaries between people dissolve, the inner and outer merge, and a new wholeness is created.

Since the mind and body are deeply linked together, such a new wholeness will also spread to the body. Holistic meaning can therefore link people at all levels, from the mental to the physical and between a person and nature. Actions, conversation, decisions, and dreams emerge out of this resonance. And clearly, synchronicity would be one manifestation of this new type of activity.

We can also envision such outflowing of meaning at even the cellular level. In an earlier section, we explored the possibility of a sort of dialogue between DNA and its surrounding environment. Within such a dialogue is also the possibility that a molecular transformation can become the appropriate response to an overall change in meaning within the environment.

But disharmonious situations also exist in which the activity of a system is at odds with its surrounding environment. For example, conflict and division experienced by an individual can give rise to a very subtle form of damage to the brain. Just as subtle structures in the brain can respond to the ever-changing field of meaning in which they are embedded, so, too, a person whose levels of meaning are incoherent and confused will develop a brain that becomes increasingly insensitive. When mind and body are no longer in harmony, confused meanings enter the body and cause illness and disease. The result is a muted response to life and even bizarre, destructive, and violent behavior.

Signals and Identity

One of the major differences between quantum theory and Einstein's theory of relativity lies in the way we think of a signal as playing an active or a passive role. Light plays a key role in Einstein's theory because while the nature of other signals depends on how fast an external observer is moving, only the properties of light remain invariant, unchanged by any form of motion. Light plays a special role in Einstein's theory. It travels at the fastest speed that anything can travel in the universe and, no matter how fast an observer moves, light always appears to be going at the same speed. For this reason, Einstein chose light, and the other frequencies of electromagnetic radiation, to define the fundamental means by which information is communicated between moving bodies and by which space-time is defined. But for a signal to have any meaning, its message must be unambiguous. In other words the signal must be clear and distinct from the body that gave rise to it. In quantum theory, however, the distinction between a signal and the quantum particles it connects is far from clear. When two quantum systems are joined by a light ray at least one indivisible quantum (a photon) must be involved. This means that no hard and fast distinction can be made between the two quantum bodies and the signal itself. In fact, they form a single, indivisible whole.

Whereas communications theory and relativity depict communication in terms of a distinct signal moving passively between two autonomous objects, quantum theory stresses the wholeness of communication. Conventional quantum theory deals in ambiguities and superpositions and does not acknowledge the essential autonomy of structures themselves. What is therefore required is a new generalization, an approach that preserves the wholeness of communication while acknowledging the coherence of collective systems.

This can be done by moving beyond the picture of a structured Hilbert space that was developed in the previous chapters. In this approach a quantum system was described by a superposition of vectors that are, however, confined within a single fixed subspace of a much larger Hilbert space. This image has already helped us explain such things as the way a crystal can grow out of its initial quantum ambiguity and attain a definite structure. It also explains how superconductors, superfluids, plasmas, and other large-scale structures or oscillations of energy have definite stable forms rather than the ambiguous superpositions implied by the paradox of Schrödinger's cat.

▇ Quantum Communication

We must now explore how such systems communicate with each other and how one system can cause a transformation or change in another. As we saw earlier, a structured quantum system can be thought of as being analogous to the occupant of a remote room along a corridor of a particular wing of an office complex. While its large-scale structure is unambiguously defined (the particular office it occupies) its microscopic structure remains ambiguous (a superposition of vectors within the subspace). Within that office, or Hilbert subspace, the quantum system is represented by an ambiguous superposition of vectors. Yet the system can never move outside this subspace, because no other vectors are available in the adjacent subspaces that can be combined with our initial vector. This new approach has enabled us to resolve such paradoxes as that of Schrödinger's cat, for now the large-scale aspects of a cooperative system can be well-defined. But in escaping from quantum ambiguity we are also in danger of falling into the grip of quantum rigidity, for unless quantum theory is changed in a radical way, our vector, or superposition of vectors, is trapped forever in its subspace, and global change is impossible. This appears to place a strict limitation on the whole idea of communication, for if a system is impervious to change, how can it enter into communication with the world around it?

Every quantum system is always defined within a particular context, for it is surrounded by a given environment. This environment may range from a physicist's laboratory to the interior of the human body, but in all cases, the description of the quantum system as a superposition of vectors within a given Hilbert subspace must always be given with respect to the particular context of its surrounding environment. Provided that the environment does not fluctuate in any essential way, the context of the description will remain fixed. Even though quantum fluctuations can take place *within* the Hilbert subspace, the overall form of the system will never change (the system never leaves its subspace).

But suppose that a major rearrangement takes place in the surrounding environment. When this happens, the whole context within which the quantum system was defined changes. For example, a fluctuation within the environment may result in an exchange of energy with the quantum system. The very indivisibility of this interaction binds quantum system and environment into an indissoluble whole. Hence, during the period of interaction, the picture of an independent quantum system in a structured Hilbert space breaks down.

Suppose that a magnetic field surrounding a superconductor is suddenly switched on, or an enzyme approaches a biological molecule in a cell. The resulting interaction means that *environment + quantum system* forms a new whole in which the original structured Hilbert space picture is submerged into a much greater *extended* Hilbert space that includes contributions (many new vectors) from the surrounding environment.

Already the connection with communication is becoming clear. The evolution of structure within a quantum system was compared earlier to the way a salt crystal emerges from a solution. To pursue the analogy further: When the surrounding environment is modified in a significant way, the result is like dissolving that crystal so that it falls back into the solution again.

Likewise, the original structured Hilbert space dissolves into a much wider Hilbert space—an extended Hilbert space that includes the whole environment. This means that the system, originally represented by a particular combination of vectors, is now free to enter into radically different combinations of vectors; indeed, it has a totally new set of vectors available with which it can mix. Our system can combine and recombine and, in this way, leapfrog into some totally new region of Hilbert space.

As the environment settles down again, and the quantum system ceases to engage in an external interaction, so, too, the original structure for Hilbert space will reemerge, as the salt crystal might crystallize out of its solution again, its same basic structure intact.

But this also allows for the system to have moved to a new subspace. The net effect is that a change in the surrounding environment permits a corresponding change in the overall structure of the quantum system. As an example, processes in the surrounding environment may modify the shape of a macromolecule, or a new set of coherent vibrations may come into existence.

Think, for example, of two large molecules A and B, located in a cell perhaps, that approach each other and begin to communicate. In isolation, each molecule has a well-defined structure. It may, for instance, have a definite shape, a particular molecular arrangement along its backbone, and collective vibrations of energy that extend throughout its length. When the molecules are very far apart, no interaction occurs, and each has its own well-defined properties. But as molecule A begins to approach molecule B, its internal collective vibrations create an interaction that can be effective a long distance away. So the coherent vibrations within molecule A affect the immediate environment of molecule B. And as the two molecules interact, it is no longer possible to consider their respective wave functions as being distinct.

Under the influence of A's energy vibrations, the original structured Hilbert space associated with B begins to dissolve into a much larger and richer Hilbert space. At one level, quantum communication therefore involves dissolution of horizons, which allows the horizon of one molecule to penetrate into that of the other. In this way, information about the collective fluctuations of A is communicated to B. The result is to induce a change in B; for example, new coherent energy pulses may be excited within that molecule. In turn, these new vibrations will be felt some distance away, around A. Now A dissolves into a new extended Hilbert space and, in the process, evolves a new structure and new excitations.

At one level, information about structure and coherent vibrations passes between the two molecules, allowing new collective oscillations to be created. But in another sense, communication involves a dissolution of form in which the two systems are constantly participating in a process of dissolution and recrystallization. One can also picture a quantum system as being in constant communication with its whole environment. Not only does the system respond to information, but by means of its own coherent vibrations, it can, in a sense, reach out and touch the environment. The long-range effects of coherent vibrations could be compared with the bursts of supersonic sound sent out by a bat as it scans the world around it. In this same way, those quantum systems connected with life can become almost prehensile through their acts of communication.

Quantum communication is a metaphor for the various complex information processes that occur at the human and social level. Clearly, all these systems involve something far more sophisticated than the passive exchange of a cargo of data. Such systems are in a state of sensitive and watchful awareness of their environment—an idea that will be taken up again in the final chapter.

Active communication is an essential feature of all life. It allows for molecules to "recognize" each other's energy patterns and undergo mutual communication. The process of enzyme recognition, for example, is of key importance in living cells. The constant pooling and exchange of information both within a cell and between that cell and its environment helps regulate and coordinate the functions of a living system.

Life is the physical manifestation of this creative flow of coherent information. Such information is active in the sense David Bohm defines it, for it binds living systems into a coherent whole and sustains their healthy functioning. When information ceases in its active role, and when its coherence breaks down, the organism enters into a state of decay and breaks up into a mere collection of inanimate components. The maintenance of a creative flow of meaning is of key importance, not only within the human body but also for the whole of society. And creativity need not be confined to the animate, for it pervades the entire natural world. In the next chapter, we shall move toward the source of this creativity and the ground of all that exists.

CHAPTER
SIX

THE HEARTBEAT OF CREATION

Over the last two hundred years, physics has painted a picture of change that depicts all forms of transformation as nothing more than a complex rearrangement or unfolding of what already exists. According to physics, every event in the universe is seen to be implicit in what has gone before and is absolutely conditioned by what precedes it. The present is always built out of the shadows of the past, and within the present is everything that will take place in the future. Scientists have a technical word for such deterministic changes; they call them *unitary transformations* and imply by this that nothing can be born into the world that is not already inherent in what exists. This assumption will be called into question in this chapter.

The concept of unitarity, or an unchanging and predictable universe, is deeply embedded within physics. In the phase space picture, knowing a single point at some time in its past enables the whole future of a system of particles to be predicted. As Laplace said, given the exact phase space coordinates of the universe at the moment of its creation, we could predict everything that will ever happen.

This picture does not really change when we move to conventional quantum theory. A quantum system is represented by a combination of vectors in Hilbert space, and Schrödinger's equation tells us how this mixture changes in time. All that is involved is a process of remixing or unitary transformation.

A unitary transformation is like a kaleidoscope in which endless patterns are produced by moving a few fragments of colored paper in front of a prism or mirror. Over a long period of time, these patterns never repeat, yet the whole history of these flowing patterns is nothing more than the permutations of a few simple elements—the pieces of colored paper. Unitary transformation can also be compared with the action of gently folding an egg into a cake batter, but with the important exception that this process could be reversed simply by turning the spoon in the opposite direction.

In quantum theory, as time moves from past to future, quantum states fold one into the other like the egg into the cake. And if the flow of time could be reversed, these states would unfold until we arrive back at the exact starting point. In one sense, "all is change," yet within this change nothing unexpected happens, for every change in a unitary universe was already totally implicit in what happened before.

■ Time in a Unitary Universe

Time in a unitary universe is static in nature. To see that this is true, compare the way time is used in physics with the pealing of a collection of bells. In many English villages, a club of enthusiasts meets on a regular basis to "ring" the bells in the tower of their local church. This belfry may contain anywhere from five to twelve bells, each sounding a different musical note. In what is called a "round" of bells, each bell is rung in a particular sequence. At the end of this round a single permutation is made by interchanging the order in which two of the bells are to be rung, and a new round is commenced. In the next "change," a further permutation is made. By ringing through all the possible permutations, what is known as "a peal of bells" is achieved. With five bells, the ringers would have to go through one hundred and twenty different permutations before coming back to the original pattern; but with twelve bells, a peal involves the astounding number of 479,001,600 changes!

Starting with a particular sequence, twelve bells could be run hour after hour, day after day, week after week, without ever repeating a given pattern of musical notes. To the casual listener, the sound of the bells is ever changing, yet while different patterns of sound are constantly being heard, each new musical phrase is already implicit in the change that was rung before. Bell ringing is a purely unitary process, for a pattern of notes that will be rung several weeks from now is an entirely predictable unfolding of the permutations that are being rung today. In fact, this whole process could equally well be rung backward as forward—it would make no difference.

All processes in a unitary universe are like this peal of bells. Events march inexorably, one into the other, ever changing yet always determined. Time, as perceived in physics, turns out to be nothing more than an ordering parameter, a measure of how much "process" has been going on. Unitary time is far closer to something that is mechanical and static than to a living, moving stream. In some ways, this manner of treating time corresponds to how a bell ringer would experience the passage of time. Locked in a bell tower, far from clocks and hard at work with the physical process of ringing, the passage of time would come to be measured by how far one had progressed along the peal. Time, as experienced within the belfry, becomes a measure of how many permutations or transformations of the original change have occurred.

Of course, given enough time, the real bell ringers would begin to feel hungry, and a variety of internal "clocks" would begin to tell their own "time." But these internal clocks are also measures of time, for they count the way internal metabolic transformations are taking place within the body.

In an analogous fashion, cooperative quantum systems, with their collective oscillations, also generate their own internal time. We measure time by electronically counting the number of oscillations within the quartz crystal of our wristwatch; in a similar fashion the "system time" of a quantum system just as a quantum "system time" relates to the number of collective oscillations or internal global transformations that take place. Time, in all these cases, is a measure of unitary transformation and unfolding.

Yet the question remains, Despite these analogies, does the idea of time as the measure of unitary transformations really capture the dynamic essence of our own experiencing of time within our lives? Can time truly be reduced to such a simple parameter? Or is it more richly experienced? Does time expand without limit? Does the mystic truly enter a timeless moment? Can we have experiences that seem to stretch across time? In what domain of time does creativity take place? Is the inscape of time truly captured as a unitary, mathematical parameter?

■ Relativistic Time

The scientific nature of time becomes even more stark in the theory of relativity. Einstein, and mathematician Hermann Minkowski, had shown that time must be added to the three dimensions of space to produce a four-dimensional space-time. Up to that point, events had been pictured as occurring in space, or in phase space, with time as the external parameter used to measure how far a point has moved along a trajectory. But in relativity, time enters on an equal footing with the other dimensions of space, and there is nothing left to "move" a point along its trajectory.

In conventional physics, a stationary stone is represented by a point A in space. In relativity theory, however, the stone occupies a location both in space and in time [Figure 6.1(a)]. Therefore, even if it is stationary in space, it is still moving through time, and in the theory of relativity, it must be pictured by a *world line* drawn in space-time. *A* is the world line of a stone at rest. *B* is the world line of a moving stone, as shown in Figure 6.1(b). Note that *B* occupies different points both in space and time.

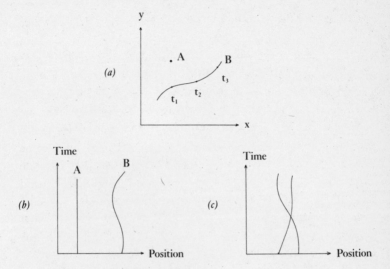

Figure 6.1. (a) The stone A is at rest. The moving stone, B, occupies different spatial positions as times t_1, t_2, t_3. (b) A space-time version of the previous diagram in which the two stones, A and B, are represented by world lines. (c) World lines for two intersecting bodies.

Figure 6.1(c) gives the world lines of a system of two particles, moving through space and time. It is also possible to draw world lines for the entire universe—a picture that would give its entire history from creation to death.

But there is something curious about all these diagrams, for they are simply networks of lines and nothing more. There is no "now" written on any one of these lines. There is no "past" and no "future." Nothing within this space-time picture describes the actual movement of a stone through space or indeed the passage of time itself, for time has now become a coordinate on the same footing as any space coordinate.

Time in Einstein's relativity is frozen. His space-time picture is not dynamic, contains no principle of generation or anything to indicate the flow from past into present. In fact, this static time has been implicit in physics for centuries, only now in Einstein's theory is it explicitly displayed in all its starkness as something remote from our own internal experience of coming into being.

▨ The Arrow of Time

Unitary time contains yet a further dilemma: The mathematical structure of unitary laws means that they are always reversible in time. In other words, the transformation from past into present can equally well be made to go in the opposite direction. So there is an essential ambiguity in the physicist's conception of time's arrow.

To take one particular example, the equations that describe the nature of light, Maxwell's equations, have two sets of solutions. If we switch on a light bulb, one of these solutions indicates that light begins within the bulb at the moment the current is switched on and then spreads outward, reaching the walls of a room a very tiny fraction of a second later. But the other, and equally valid, solution says that light is already at the walls of the room a tiny fraction of a second *before* the current is switched on. This light collapses inward and arrives at the filament of the bulb at the exact instant the switch is thrown. This second set of solutions is like a movie film of the first set that has been projected in reverse. Or to put it another way, the second set of solutions is exactly like the first set but with time going backward!

What is true for Maxwell's equations is equally true for the other fundamental laws of physics, for there is no way, within the context of that particular law, to determine which direction of time (past into future or future into past) is correct. Time is always reversible in physics, and physicists are forced to make the additional *assumption* that time flows from past to future. They then use this assumption to select "real" solutions from those that are "unphysical."

But on what basis is this assumption made? Is there anything within the theory itself that gives a reason for picking one direction of time over another? The idea of an arrow of time is certainly very real to us in our daily lives. But when it comes to physics, does this arrow have a real existence, or is it simply the result of some convention or a psychological quirk of our consciousness?

Physicists have attempted to come to grips with the ambiguity of time's direction by proposing, for example, that it is the actual Big Bang creation of the universe and its subsequent expansion that singles out one temporal direction, or that a unique flow of time begins at the quantum level. But this question cannot really be answered within the confines of a unitary universe it demands that we move into a new, nonunitary world.

■ A Nonunitary Universe

For two centuries, physics has assumed that every change that takes place in the universe can be looked on as the result of a unitary process. But what if unitary processes are only special cases of something much wider? What if the most basic transformations in the universe are essentially *nonunitary*?

Immediately when we go beyond the world of unitary transformations, we realize that totally novel sorts of processes are possible—processes, for example, that unfold elements that are in no way implicit in anything that has gone before. Nonunitary transformations allow for the totally new to enter the universe and imply that the future is not entirely contained, or enfolded, within the present. Nonunitary transformations mean that knowing the entire past history of a system may not be sufficient to determine, absolutely, its next instant. Nonunitary processes allow freedom to enter the universe and limit the grip of determinism.

Since science has conditioned us to think in terms of unitary transformations and a limited notion of time, it is difficult suddenly to abandon that approach and begin thinking in new nonunitary ways. But a simple analogy can be given. To return to those bell ringers, suppose they live with the constant possibility that a new bell will be added to the belfry. When this happens, the whole nature of the permutations is altered in a discontinuous way. Once an extra bell has been added, there will exist changes that could never have been rung or even anticipated in the past.

The addition of a new bell also establishes an absolute separation in time. Up to that point, the present was always contained implicitly within the past and made manifest through a series of unitary transformations (the permutations of the bells). But with a new bell in the belfry, the future will be absolutely distinguished from the past. Indeed, no unitary transformation, no permutation of the original set of bells, can ever produce this new pattern of notes. Whereas in a unitary belfry it is possible to reverse the direction of time simply by ringing the changes in reverse order, in a nonunitary belfry there will be an absolute arrow of time—a separation of past from future.

The universe can, therefore, be compared with a belfry in which new bells are constantly being added, a universe in which time moves uniquely from past to future and in which the next moment can never be fully predicted, even given absolute knowledge of the past.

Nonunitary Quantum Theory

Like other fundamental theories of physics, quantum theory has always been treated as unitary. For example, the equations developed by Schrödinger and by Heisenberg employ unitary transformations to change quantum states in time. But with the new ideas of structured Hilbert spaces, it is now possible to discuss the idea of nonunitary quantum processes directly.

In the last chapter, I proposed that quantum systems cooperatively evolve their own structures, which is reflected in a correspondingly richly structured Hilbert space. To this extent, while individual quantum fluctuations and ambiguities are still permitted *within* the Hilbert subspace, the collective structure of a quantum system itself remains stable and well defined. While it is possible for macromolecules, superconductors, and other large-scale quantum systems to change their overall structures through a process analogous to communication, the idea of a spontaneous jump from one Hilbert subspace to another is strictly forbidden. Indeed, an axiom embedded deep within the mathematics of quantum theory states that no unitary process will ever be able to move a quantum system from one subspace to another. But once we realize that unitary processes are only special cases of something more general, nonunitary transformations, then quantum systems can undergo spontaneous evolution and modification.

In the previous chapter, we saw how the long-range interactions of one system could influence the Hilbert space of another. When a quantum system enters into communication with some other system, its structured Hilbert space actually dissolves into an extended Hilbert space. In essence, communication becomes communion as each system dissolves into the environment provided by the other. Following this, the systems recrystallize again and show a modification of their original global structure.

But we are now about to enter a nonunitary world that goes even beyond this, for in a nonunitary transformation, a quantum system dissolves into a world of novelty and potentiality. With each nonunitary transformation, Hilbert space dissolves and re-forms. And with each transformation, radical change, evolution, and modification become possible. A nonunitary transformation could be pictured, for example, as allowing a quantum system access to totally new vectors that have never existed in that Hilbert space before. Within a nonunitary transformation, a quantum system opens itself to true novelty.

▓ The Heartbeat of the Universe

Quantum mechanics is only one particular theory of physics, and, as I have suggested in this book, no theory can ever be definitive or offer a complete description of one of nature's levels. Therefore, to apply nonunitary ideas to quantum theory alone does not go far enough. In fact, the very idea of nonunitarity goes beyond any particular physical theory, for it involves a totally new way of looking at the universe and a radically different way of experiencing becoming and being in time.

Once nonunitarity is admitted into the universe, we lose that hard and fast division between the animate and the inanimate, between the material and the infinitely subtle, for the whole of existence is now no longer fixed and solid; rather, it has a sort of flickering existence.

A nonunitary transformation takes us from the present into a future that is no longer a deterministic unfolding of what is already present but is unknown and totally open. It may well be that the future contains echoes and memories of the present and that certain tendencies in the past continue to unfold into the future. Nevertheless, this future is truly free and unlimited; it is never absolutely conditioned by the past; there is always a possibility for the new, the novel, and the unexpected to emerge.

As to the actual nonunitary transformation itself, it can be thought of as bringing about the dissolution of all forms and structures. Just as the structured Hilbert space of a quantum system that enters into communion with another will dissolve into something that is beyond itself, so, too, within a nonunitary transformation, the processes, forms, and structure of the world cease to be. Within that transformation, the universe touches what could be called a ground of unconditioned creativity. Then, as the present re-forms again—this present that lies in the future—the world and all its forms and structures recrystallize.

The nonunitary world is indeed like a crystal. It comes into existence out of a matrix of possibilities. Yet unlike a single crystal of salt or quartz, the universe is in a constant process of crystallization and dissolution. At each instant the rock, the tree, the atom, the star, and the human mind die and are born anew.

The universe is eternally fresh—like a baker's loaf hot from the oven. Each day loaves are sold at the baker's, and each day they smell fresh and appetizing, yet there is a continuity of form and texture about the bread. The bread is simultaneously new, yet it is the same physical manifestation of a lifelong skill and tradition.

The meaning and implications of nonunitarity are so radical that at present it is only possible to talk about them in terms of metaphors and allusions. As an example, the constant coming into existence and dissolution of the nonunitary universe could be compared with a beating heart or with the ever-repeating cycle of birth and death. This pattern of birth and death applies as much to a molecule or a stone as it does to a single thought or a whole human life. Indeed, the distinction between the animate and the inanimate has begun to dissolve, for everything is involved in a pattern of continuous rebirth, and everything is the manifestation of one underlying creative potential. Synchronicity, at this level, is a bubbling up of ever-fresh forms, patterns, and connections that transcend all boundaries between mind and matter, the physical and the spiritual.

The cycle of dissolution and recrystallization that characterizes everything that exists within a nonunitary world does, however, pose a challenge: If the universe dissolves at each instant, where does it go? What in fact lies between the instants of the heartbeats of nature? It is not really possible to give a straightforward discursive answer to this question. Everything we can say about form, structure, and order belongs to the world of manifest reality, the world of crystallized form. At present, science has no words for what could lie beyond this. The interval bridged by a nonunitary transformation lies outside everything that is known to science as it is presently practiced.

Indeed, to speak of a "ground of unconditioned creativity" is in itself misleading. The very idea of a ground summons up all kinds of images and parallels that belong to the world of the known and the structured. The word *ground*, being a noun, conveys the sense of some sort of existence or being in time. To talk of "unconditioned process" is no better, for it implies activity and evokes the ideas of change and transformation that lie within the world of time. Indeed, what may lie beyond the manifest moment in time seems more properly to belong to the world of the mystic rather than to the physicist or philosopher.

To give an illustration, imagine an object reflected by a magical mirror and suppose that the world of the reflection is as real as that of the original object. The mirror is a transformation that takes an object from one world into another, yet the mirror itself is not a part of either world; it is the active membrane that lies between them both and connects them. The mirror is an active participant in both worlds while belonging to neither.

This ancient image of a speculum or mirror, a device that links two worlds and belongs to neither, was of great importance in the thinking of physicist Wolfgang Pauli. The speculum, he believed, holds an important clue to the inner nature of reality. Likewise, in the case of a nonunitary universe, what lies between each moment of existence, the speculum or mirror, can never be described or contained within the world of the known and the experienced.

■ The Spirit Breathing

Nonunitary transformations break a pattern of thinking that stretches back to the ideas of Newton, Galileo, and Descartes, a way of thinking that has spread from the physical sciences to cast its influence over so many other fields of study. Nonunitary transformations represent a new, and hitherto unexplored, frontier in science. They can, for example, lead to totally new insights in quantum theory, for we have already seen how, under the influence of successive nonunitary transformations, a structured Hilbert space constantly dissolves and recrystallizes.

This whole approach also connects to ideas that are extremely ancient. The wisdom traditions of many peoples teach of the ephemeral nature of the material world and that all existence is of a flickering nature. But the image of a heartbeat, of something that moves in and out of existence through a series of pulses, also evokes the notion of a nonunitary transformation that is applied to a structured Hilbert space. At each heartbeat of the transformation, Hilbert space dissolves into a deeper ground and then reforms and recrystallizes. This image connects an ancient philosophy to a frontier idea in physics.

Another ancient image is that of breathing. Breath animates the body and gives it life. Throughout the world, a variety of practices that increase awareness of the way breath enters and leaves the body bring one in direct contact with breath's animating principle. In such traditional practices, breath is not simply a physical manifestation; it is a rhythm that permeates the whole organism and connects it to the rhythms of the cosmos. It is the intaking of the spirit into matter. Indeed, breathing spirit into matter is a widespread image for the creator of life and the universe.

Both in the ancient wisdom traditions and now, as a metaphor for nonunitary transformations, matter receives its animation through breathing. Yet this same breath must also be exhaled and the principle of life withdrawn. Similarly, the nonunitary universe is involved, at each moment, in a constant cycle of birth and death. There can be no becoming without a corresponding ceasing to be. And as the sections that follow will reveal, there must also be a process of clinging contained within the cycle of birth and death.

Time and the Moment

Faced with the mystery of a universe in a continuous process of creation and death, it is natural to ask, What happens within this magical instant in which the universe ceases to exist? Such an instant lies totally outside time. Time, as we saw, involves process—the ticking of a clock, the oscillation of a quartz crystal in a watch, the cycles of day and night, the movements of the seasons. In physics, time is a measure of how many unitary transformations have taken place and how far a particular implication has unfolded.

But clearly, none of these processes is present when the structure of the universe dissolves and comes in contact with, for want of a better description (and with great reservation), what we will call its *creative source*. Time at that point ends. There is no moment and no time within a nonunitary transformation, for time only has meaning within the processes of the manifest unitary world, and the nonstate of dissolution lies outside time.

The meaning of a nonunitary transformation, therefore, is for the universe to leave time and to cease to have any existence within the realm of the known. Following that transformation, the world recrystallizes again and reenters the domain of time. As the mystics of old well knew, material existence lives in time, but its roots lie elsewhere.

One way of approaching the idea of a nonunitary transformation is to see it as a process whereby the present is moved into the future. But a deeper view would be that this transformation creates an eternal yet ever-changing now. We exist in the present, and this present constantly dissolves and reforms anew. Time is no longer a river; it is a dynamic bubbling spring whose waters are ever fresh. Existence is a series of stepping stones of time. Each island is called "the present" and lies in an ocean beyond time and structure.

A nonunitary universe demands a radically new vision of time, one that makes a deeper connection with our own immediate experience, for we do not so much travel through time in our lives as we live in an eternal but ever-changing now. Our experience is always immediate and direct; we never feel, for example, that we must make an effort to move through time in the same way that we travel through space. No matter what we do within the present, tomorrow will always come, no sooner and no later.

Existence belongs to the interval between transformations, as the transformation itself takes us outside time. There is no temporal interval, no gap in time, between one "now" and the next. Moments of timefulness are like the stones of an ancient building laid so close together that nothing can be placed between them. There is "no thing" between one timeful moment and the next, for all that exists lies within the domain of time, and non-unitary processes take us outside that domain. The flickering of the universe therefore involves moments that are both infinitely close and yet unbridgeable by any unitary transformation.

Time Beyond Dimension

Time in physics is traditionally treated as a dimension analogous to the dimensions of space. Indeed, time is the additional dimension that must be added to make up the four-dimensional space-time of Einstein's relativity. But already we can see that in a nonunitary universe time must be far richer than this.

To begin with, an absolute distinction now exists between past and future. Unitary transformations, for their part, work equally well in reverse and are unable to define an arrow of time. But by their very nature, nonunitary transformations can never be reversed; they uniquely take the known past into the open future. To borrow from Thomas Wolfe, "You can't go home again." The past is absolutely distinguished from the future; it can never be regained, and time assumes a unique direction of flow.

As we begin to strip away the assumptions that have restricted the physicist's conception of time, we reveal something that is far closer to our own experience. Epiphanies, for example, tell us directly how a transcendent perception can move beyond all structure and form to enter the timeless moment. Synchronicities speak to us of patterns unconfined by the constraints of time, space, and causality. At the deepest moments of our lives, we are not trapped by the linear, dimensional, mechanical time of physics but feel free to enter a much greater pool of being.

Time and Time Again

In the new version of quantum theory we are exploring here, nonunitary time moves beyond the confines of a single parameter or dimension. Time appears to play two sorts of roles in the nonunitary version of quantum theory. At one level, time functions as the conventional temporal measure that is still reversible and relatively mechanical. This sort of time is involved in the way quantum states mix *within* a Hilbert subspace. It is a measure of the extent to which unitary processes have been going on in the system. This time appears as parameter t in Schrödinger's equation and has traditionally been equated with "time" itself.

In prequantum physics, the reversible, mathematical time expressed how far a particle had moved along a phase space trajectory, and in relativity theory, time becomes just another coordinate axis in the grid of space-time. But another aspect of time enters our new formulation of quantum theory, one that is related to the nonunitary transformations themselves. Whereas unitary time is a measure of the mixing of states, nonunitary time is concerned with dissolution and recrystallization of Hilbert space structure. It is a mirror that takes the now and reflects it into a free and open future. This aspect of time was earlier compared with the heartbeats of the universe or with the ticking of the cosmic clock. So in order to understand quantum theory properly, we must approach time from two directions, or focus on time in two of its many aspects. This is not to say that time itself is fragmented—simply that our formulation and discourse have abstracted two particular sides to the rich nature of time.

The idea of time and timelessness represents one of the truly great mysteries of nature. Even this present discussion is nothing more than a new scratch on the surface of time. But at least it is now clear that the domain of time goes far beyond the conception of dimensionality or Einstein's simple space-time. We must therefore go back over two hundred years and reconsider the philosopher Descartes's attempt to quantify all experience. After all, it is but a short step from the idea of Cartesian coordinates to that of time as a regular mathematical order or a parameter in a mathematical equation. By restricting time in this way, the map of the universe became impoverished, and one of the most subtle of our experiences, time, was devalued. Only now, with a new nonunitary vision, is it possible to reinstate the essential mystery of time.

The Universe as a Work of Art

Nonunitary transformations can revitalize the maps of science by bringing them closer to human experience. Synchronicities and epiphanies were earlier banished from the phase space map with its absolute determinism and objectivity. And in eliminating the whole mystery and quality of life, the maps of science moved closer to the planes of elaborate and complex machines and away from their earlier sense of communion with the natural world.

Since a nonunitary transformation lies beyond anything that is conditioned or absolutely bound to the past, it raises a significant question: Why is there something rather than nothing? Why are there forms and structures, worlds and thoughts, memories and experiences, rather than an amorphous, featureless, flickering now? After all, each moment is born anew out of a nonunitary transformation that lies beyond the conditioning of the past. So why should there be any continuity in the universe, and why should anything be recognizable from one instant to the next?

Nonunitary science moves beyond the current goal of science to explain matter in terms of ever smaller and ever more fundamental laws, for each level is complete in itself and participates in the same creative ground. The universe comes closer to a work of art, a painting, a symphony, or a cosmic dance than to a great and complex machine. And it is through this metaphor of a work of art that we may begin to sense why there can be order within this bubbling lifespring of creativity.[1]

Listen to a symphony, and you enter a new world that unfolds before you: It grows and develops; it is peopled by ever more detailed structures; excursions are made; and tensions are built up and resolved. The symphony is an interplay of themes and rhythms, emotions, sensations, and logical structures. On the one hand, the symphony is free and creative, for it holds its secrets to the last note. Yet, on the other hand, the symphony is also concerned with order and structure. Themes and rhythms interplay within each movement, and the movements themselves resonate and reflect each other. A symphony is both richly structured and ever fresh. If a symphony were musically determinate and predictable, it would bore us and leave us emotionally cold. On the other hand, if it simply meandered and followed every musical whim, it would be without interest or challenge. A symphony therefore explores the tensions between freedom and constraint, and as with all great works of art, it has the effect on the listener of binding sensation, intellect, emotion, and perception together and making them whole.

Yet these orders and structures are not imposed in an arbitrary fashion from outside, but emerge organically and perfectly naturally from the music itself—and indeed from the whole language of music. The same is true of a painting or a dance. In each case, orders unfold organically and bind the work together. They are never absolute, for they depend on the wider context of the whole work, and if that context should change, the orders, laws, and structures are themselves modified.

So the order of a work of art emerges out of the very process of its creation and feeds back to unify and hold the evolving work together. At every instant, there is an interplay between the order of a piece and its unfoldment to the listener. Now imagine a symphony without end, a symphony of the universe, one that is ever fresh and whose unifying forms and structures are never absolute. This is the essence of a nonunitary universe.

▮ Clinging to Form

Just as a work of art evolves its own forms, so, too, structures in the universe contain recurring themes and patterns. To the duality of birth and death must now be added a tendency of clinging to form and the persistence of matter. Within the creative moment of every nonunitary transformation, there is the possibility that certain forms may be reborn and enter back into themselves. The unitary therefore forms a special, limited case of the nonunitary, and it is this aspect that is responsible for regularity within the universe.

The electron is forever being born, yet in its very birth, there is a tendency for its form to be regenerated. Similarly, when a Native American talks to a rock, he or she is seeing beyond its inertia and responding to the very aliveness in all things, to the infinite richness and integrity of all levels of existence. At one level, the rock and the electron represent stability, the unchanging, concrete manifestation of habitual matter. Yet at another, each is the very vibration of the universe and emerges at every instant new born and unique yet with a form that is always similar to itself. The rock and the electron—each never the same yet ever abiding in its form.

■ Natural Law

The presence of unitarity and clinging within the creative play of the universe is the deeper meaning that lies behind physical law. It is the essence of Newton's great discovery, for clinging need not simply refer to the stability of a physical structure. It can also include the whole manner of an object's being within the world, such as the way it moves through space. Newton's First Law of Motion says that a system, totally isolated from all external effects, will persist in what it is already doing. Not only does a rock cling to the form of a rock, but its motion is sustained. The rock continues to move in the same direction and at exactly the same speed, and the First Law is a law of the clinging, or unitarity, within the heart of change; it tells us that being persists in itself within the very process of continuous birth. Newton called the continuance of motion *inertia*, and now we see that inertia is a form of clinging, the habitual process whereby a body always manifests its motion in a similar way.

Newton's Second Law deals with the way that this clinging

is broken. Yet whenever a force induces a change in motion, it does so in such a way that motion clings to the change itself. So when the force of gravity acts to pull an apple, or the moon, toward the earth, it pulls motion away from its First Law clinging but in such a way that even this deviation produces a new order of clinging, for at each instant, the change in velocity is the same (acceleration is constant).

Unitarity clinging also enters Einstein's theory of relativity. But now rather than clinging to motion itself, nature clings to the very *form* of change. Understanding this can help us toward obtaining a wider picture of natural law.

Einstein had pointed out that observers who move at different speeds, close to that of light, experience things in quite different ways. But if appearances are different for different observers, Einstein asked, then how can there be any objective order to the world? The answer is to see beyond appearance to the underlying stability of order, that is, to a clinging to form within the very laws themselves. While the *appearance* of a particular phenomenon may depend on the motion of an observer, Einstein concluded in his special theory of relativity of 1905, the underlying *laws* are always the same. The laws are objective and do not depend on the way in which any particular observer happens to move.

Suppose that a group of scientists carry out experiments inside a high-speed rocket far out in space. Given time, they begin to discover the basic laws of nature. Another group of scientists, in a rocket traveling at a very different speed, see quite different phenomena and formulate the laws of nature in their own terms. For example, what appears to one set of observers to be the effects of an electrical current may appear to someone who moves at a different speed to be a magnetic phenomenon. But Einstein discovered a way of writing down generalizations of these laws in such a way that they remain the same, no matter how fast an observer happens to be moving. Newton stressed the law of inertia or clinging to motion, and now Einstein went deeper by proposing that there is even an inertia to the laws themselves. So while scientists who work in laboratories that travel at different speeds see phenomena in different ways, they are nonetheless able to agree on the basic laws of nature.

A decade later, Einstein faced the problem of a different class of observers, those who undergo high acceleration or who live in an intense gravitational field. Sealed up in a windowless rocket, a scientist notices that apples and feathers fall to the floor at the same rate. Does this mean that the rocket is standing on earth or constantly accelerating away from earth? What looks to one observer like a change of speed can appear to someone else as the force of gravity.

In the general theory of relativity, Einstein discovered that his earlier (special relativity) formulation was not general enough to account for such a paradox. It now appeared that the very language in which the laws of physics are written—mathematical expressions using coordinates in space-time—changes from observer to observer. Mathematical laws for motion in empty space look quite different from the laws close to a black hole or in a rapidly accelerating spaceship.

Up to that time, the laws of nature had been written using Cartesian coordinates, assuming that the surrounding space has the normal flat geometry first discussed by Euclid. But what if geometry itself depends on gravity and acceleration? What if space-time is curved? Under such conditions, the mathematical expression of laws of nature appears different in regions of different curvature.

And so Einstein was forced to look even deeper for uniformity in nature. His great insight, called the general theory of relativity, was that the particular *details* of a mathematical expression are not as important as its overall *form*. The laws of nature, Einstein argued, must be written in such a way that their *form* is identical no matter how space and time are distorted. That is, the laws must be independent of all coordinate systems because, while a particular law may look different, when it is transformed from one space-time geometry to another, its overall form must remain unchanged.

Within the creativity of the universe, forms, orders, and laws tend to return into themselves. This clinging applies both to material structures and to the ways in which they move and change. Even space itself becomes the clinging form of a particular ordered set of relationships. Both space and matter are constantly being dissolved and re-created, and within this process of change is something that clings and returns to itself. Just as time has been radically transformed in a nonunitary universe, so the whole idea of space may go far beyond such simple notions as dimensionality and locality.

■ The Orders of Space

Each level and aspect of nature unfolds out of a nonunitary transformation, and its very essence ranges from the clinging and unitary to the creative and unlimited. This gives us a whole new way of looking at the idea of space. Space at one level is a set of relationships that are always similar to themselves, but it may also go beyond the restrictions of location. The orders of space may reflect back on themselves at a wide variety of scales so that processes at the astronomical level connect directly with those at the subatomic. Space may also possess the properties of what is called nonlocality, so that direct connections can exist between distant objects.

Nonlocality is a puzzling idea that physicists have recently been forced to confront, partly as the result of an astonishing theorem of the late John Bell.[2] Objects in the classical world can be connected if they are in direct contact with each other, or if they are linked, like a magnet and a compass needle, by a force field. But in this latter case, the strength of the connection gets weaker, the greater the separation. Not so with nonlocality. In quantum theory, quite distant objects seem to be connected directly. John Bell showed that if two photons or two electrons are allowed to separate to opposite sides of a laboratory, they will still be actively correlated. Moreover, the connection between them is direct and instantaneous and is not the result of some mysterious force or field.

Clearly, John Bell's nonlocal correlations demand a richer structure to space and the notion of separation. While Bell's result applies only to the world of quantum theory, I am suggesting here that it is a manifestation of a much wider principle of non-locality. But, since our thinking is so strongly tied to a conventional picture of space, it is not easy to change our usual notions of distance. Think of two knots on a piece of string. They may be very far apart when that string is stretched on the ground, but tangle that string and the knots now come into contact. So depending on how you measure distance, along the length of the string or by a more direct route, the knots could be well separated or in contact. In a similar way, many orders within space may be in direct contact with other orders.

Opening the door on the rich and subtle properties of space allows for all kinds of novel interconnections within the universe. Perhaps, for example, nonlocal connections join every part of the universe, so that orders are everywhere repeated. This would explain why elementary particles like electrons, neutrons, protons, mesons, and so on, are everywhere the same, so that a uniformity of nature extends across the universe.

Extreme regularity also appears within the large-scale structure of the universe, and this poses a compelling puzzle. Current theories suggest that the early expansion of the universe was so rapid that, within a short time, parts of the universe became spatially separated so as to be beyond direct interaction. According to the theory of relativity, signals that carry information about one region of the universe to another cannot exceed the speed of light. So in a rapidly expanding universe, this information would not have time to reach a distant region before that region had expanded far away. In the absence of such connections, there is no reason why different parts of the universe should not have begun to go their separate ways, each evolving slightly differently.

As an illustration, our earth once consisted of a giant protocontinent that later split up and drifted across the globe. It surprises no one that animals in the various continents should be so different, because they have evolved independently. One would expect something similar to have happened to the universe itself, yet results from NASA's *Cosmic Background Explorer* indicate that the cosmic background radiation in the universe is astonishingly uniform and that even three hundred thousand years after the Big Bang, the density of matter in all the universe was uniform to an accuracy of well over one part in ten thousand.

One explanation for this uniformity is that a direct connection exists between even the most remote parts of the universe. Or to put it another way, a clinging to form would embrace the various global and local structures of space, together with the elementary particles and forces of nature. An interpenetrating clinging would provide the uniformity seen in nature.

This clinging to form could also occur at different scales of size to form resonances and interconnections between them. It is indeed curious that forms and patterns do appear to repeat themselves at all scales from the submicroscopic to the astronomical. This suggests that direct connections may exist between different levels of scale and distance.

■ Rupert Sheldrake, Morphic Fields, and Unitarity

We have seen that the laws of the universe are no longer absolute but always depend on a deeper context. The controversial idea that laws of nature are accumulated habits has been explicitly proposed by biologist Rupert Sheldrake. At first sight, his idea that a law is a habit may appear similar to the suggestion within this book that laws are the descriptions of material patterns of clinging. However, there are a number of important differences between the ideas explored in this book and Sheldrake's proposal. Most significantly, his whole theory of guiding fields of habit is formulated from within a strictly unitary picture of the world and using a conventional view of time.

Sheldrake's morphic fields (fields of habit) can be understood with the help of the biologist Conrad Hall Waddington's image of a developing organism being like a ball rolling down a hill. As an embryo grows, it is perturbed by a wide variety of contingencies from within its environment. Yet time and time again, and in a wide variety of different environments, embryos grow into fully functioning adults. Likewise, a variety of animals survive injury, repair themselves, and even, in some cases, develop missing limbs. Sheldrake even points out that a crystal of a particular substance, grown anywhere in the world, always shows its perfect form.

If a developing organism is compared with a ball rolling along a landscape, then, as Sheldrake points out, we must also take into account the contingencies of life, the chance bumps, hollows, and tiny diversions within that landscape. In his opinion, something must be added to the conventional forces of nature—a guiding field, called a morphic field.

In the case of a crystal, for example, the first time a totally new substance is synthesized, it does not possess a morphic field but crystallizes out in response to the conventional forces of nature, with each atom responding to a particular push or pull. Anecdotal information suggests that this first act of crystallization is incredibly slow and difficult to achieve but that subsequent crystallizations become quicker and easier. Sheldrake's proposal is that each time the crystal forms, it reinforces a field of habit. In turn, this field acts to guide the incoming atoms that make up the next crystal. Although atoms move in response to conventional electromagnetic forces, they are also being guided by a field of habit. Moreover, Sheldrake's morphic fields appear to transcend the normal limits of space, for the morphic field of a crystal first synthesized in Berlin, for example, will then act to guide a subsequent crystallization in New York.

Sheldrake's morphic fields are, he proposes, responsible not only for the growth of a crystal or an embryo but for the instinctual responses of animals, even for the ease with which humans develop skills such as riding a bicycle or typing. As more and more people throughout the world ride bicycles, he argues, it becomes easier to learn, because the field of habit is constantly being strengthened and reinforced.

Sheldrake's ideas are provocative and stimulating. It is always useful to have someone question the prevailing scientific paradigm. But I feel that his idea of a morphic field is not clear, and his underlying arguments do not really go far enough. The present objections are therefore offered out of respect to Sheldrake and as a stimulant to further debate.

To begin with, Sheldrake accepts the current scientific vision in which organisms and complex structures are always seen in terms of simpler and smaller components, the difference now being that the way these components fit together is guided by a morphic field. This hierarchical picture of nature even applies to the morphic fields themselves, for the morphic field of an organism contains within it a field for individual organs, which itself contains fields for cells, complex molecules, and so on. Indeed, morphic fields now become an image of the supposed hierarchical structure of the material world.

Thus, in order to explain the stability of matter, an infinity of additional fields has to be admitted into physics. But in this book I have argued that stable structures and processes are complete in themselves. They are examples of collective, cooperative behavior and of an active dialogue or communion with the environment.

Sheldrake's fields, however, preserve a troublesome duality. On the one hand, they are distinct from matter and from more conventional fields such as gravity and electromagnetism, for they represent a new addition to physics. Yet, on the other hand, they act directly to change the mechanical motions and arrangements of matter. It is not at all clear how these morphic fields interact with matter or how they are built up and reinforced by material forms. Are they energy-carrying fields like the other fields of physics? If so, they require the definition of new forces and new forms of interaction. But if this is so, then how is it that their strength does not fall off with distance and time as is the case with other fields? And if they have nothing to do with the conventional fields of matter and somehow transcend the limitations of space, how exactly do they operate and by what means do they interact with material forms and become reinforced by them?

As fields of habit, they differ from the notion of clinging that has been introduced in this book. Matter and material processes, I have proposed, have a tendency to cling to form within the general nonunitarity of change. This clinging is a generalization of the whole idea of inertia and is not the result of some field or force that is *external* to matter itself. Clinging, I suggest, is the very nature of matter, for "that which clings" is another name for the material, and these patterns of clinging are what we refer to as physical laws. By contrast, Sheldrake's external morphic fields are built up over time and act on matter as agents. Habit or a clinging to form is not, in Sheldrake's opinion, inherent to matter but requires the activity of external morphic fields. The laws of nature appear, in his view, to be built up in time and constantly reinforced by themselves.

Sheldrake's fields are therefore based within a unitary vision of nature and tied to a vision of evolutionary process in time. It takes time to build up habits, and these habits, it appears, evolve their complexity over time in a fashion. By contrast, the ideas of time presented in this book are more complex: At one level, material forms do appear to evolve in time; at another, they can be viewed as unfolding outside this dimension of time.

In a unitary world, it is difficult to see how anything truly novel can emerge. This is the problem Sheldrake faces, for how are the morphic fields for an entirely new species created? Are they nothing more than the rearrangement or modification of some already existing field, or has some new assumption to be made about morphic fields? In a nonunitary world, however, the emergence of totally new forms presents no problem; indeed, they can also be seen as the creative response to an ongoing dialogue within the natural world.[3]

▇ Remembrance of Things Past

To recognize the world as nonunitary is to have a profoundly different attitude toward such ideas as knowledge and control, and this is tied to the whole notion of what constitutes the past. It is sometimes said that a particular person is "living in the past." And just as an individual may be in the grips of memories, repressions, and habitual neuroses, so, too, in a unitary universe, the past exists in an enfolded way within the present. But once we acknowledge that the universe is essentially nonunitary, we are forced to accept that the past is dead.

Since our memories and evocations of the past are so vivid, it will come as a great shock to learn that the past has no real existence. What we call the past is really a creation or projection from within the present. Within a nonunitary world, the past is truly dead; the future does not exist, and only the present is real.

But what does it mean to say that the past has no real existence? Think of your own memories. Cast your mind back to a particular memory of childhood or of a first love. If you examine this memory very carefully, you will realize that it is really a recreation that is colored by the present. The evocations of events that happened earlier in life are always created, within the present, out of the various memories and records held in the brain. At the same time, however, they are colored by our present attitudes and beliefs.

Suppose, for example, that you were to learn something unsavory about a prominent figure in your childhood. Your memory of that person would suddenly be changed. Of course, the way you recall their face and physical stance will be the same, but the whole flavor of the memory will have been transformed. It is also revealing to go back to a location you have not seen since childhood. To see that stream or tree or deserted barn where you used to play can be a profound shock. It simply does not look right—indeed, one almost prefers the power of a cherished memory to the harsh facts of everyday reality. Memory is a construct that is constantly colored by our present wishes, desires, nostalgia, knowledge, and attitudes.

In this sense, the only reality that the past can ever have lies within the present, for the present breathes life into the past. Pick up a book containing a favorite poem and reread it. No matter how many times you have looked at that poem before, it will always be new. Each time you read the poem, it comes alive, its metaphors hold new levels of meaning, and its imagery evokes new feelings and sensations. Each time you pick up that poem, you are a new person who brings fresh thoughts and experience to the reading. In a similar way, a historian who attempts to re-create a battle is always aware that this "reality" is a product of the present time with all its political interests and particular concerns.

This is the essence of the past. In itself, it has no true existence. To speak of the past is therefore to evoke, out of the memories, fossils and other physical records held by the physical world, a particular existence within the living present. In this sense, the past is forever born anew.

What is true for human memory is also true of the physical world, and this casts new light on the whole meaning of physical laws. For all that exists, in a certain sense, lies in the present, and within the context of that present, science, through its laws, attempts to evoke the past and anticipate the future. Yet time past and time future are ephemeral because in a nonunitary universe only the present is real.

It is certainly true, however, that mechanical forms and processes, like the swing of a pendulum and the structure of a rock, obey unitary laws and arise out of themselves in a deterministic and conditioned way. In this sense, the past is mechanically carried into the present, and the present into the future. But since unitary transformations are always special, limited cases of the nonunitary, it is more correct to say that the past and the future are unfolded in a unitary fashion out of the implications of the present.

So the present contains the past, but only as it is enfolded within all manner of unitary processes, records, fossils, muscular tensions within the bodies, tendencies for motion to continue along its present course. In short, the aspects of nature's clinging carry with them echoes and shadows of the past.

Likewise, it is possible to anticipate the future, for certain of its tendencies are held, enfolded, within the unitary processes of the present. One can predict the appearance of an eclipse for many centuries into the future or calculate the instant at which a space probe will enter into orbit around a distant planet. But always, such unitary processes are limiting cases; they apply only within certain boundaries and contexts, which themselves are always open to change.

In a more fundamental sense, the future does not exist—it cannot be reached in any unitary way from within the present. All science can do is to create an image of the future, within our present, by unfolding the tendencies to cling within the unitary processes of nature. We anticipate this future. We hold an image of that future within our minds. And so we enter into the whole paradox of time, for as nonunitary transformations take us into the future "now," we take with us that created image, which now becomes a memory. And in tomorrow's "now," we hold a memory of what we once believed that tomorrow to be!

Science therefore becomes a process of comparing memories with actuality. It is a world of shadows and shadows of shadows. And within that new world, the whole notion of the control of nature assumes a radically different meaning, for our attitude toward the future and its prediction is closer to an intelligent art than to the certainty of a rigid mechanical scheme.

▪ Human Thought and Scientific Order

The notion of the unreality of the past causes us to examine the laws of nature once again. We realize that within a nonunitary universe no absolute laws lie outside nature or have existence before matter, space, and time. Rather, laws unfold out of the creative flux of the world. They are the patterns, forms, and invariants that science has used to create unity within the rich diversity of the manifest world.

Yet science is the creation of the human scientist, and historically, its explorations began through the agency of our physical bodies and the particular range of our senses. The first levels of patterns and invariants that science settled on, those clinging to form, were a reflection of the range and structure of our senses and the scale of our physical interactions with the world. New scientific instruments enabled us to extend those senses and to reveal yet wider patterns within the flux of the material world.

Physics, with its concern for order in the natural world, may have extended the details of the recurrence and stability of material objects, regularities of motion, and the patterns of change. But the essence of the universe goes far beyond this, for the world of regularity and simple orders is only a tiny fraction of everything that exists. Indeed, any order that the mind can conceive must be limited, because there will always be something that is nonunitary, free, and creative and lies beyond any order. Physics is therefore concerned with only a tiny island of regularity within a much greater ocean of infinite complexity and creativity, and its maps can never be complete or fully satisfying at the human level.

Human thought picks out from the infinite flux of the universe those processes and structures whose orders are similar to itself. The mind makes a mental image of its own order and takes it for the whole of reality. And so consciousness abstracts from the bubbling, buzzing confusion of the world material structures, patterns, forms, and laws that are in fact a mirror of its own unitary activity! But any fixed order that thought can conceive is limited. Other forms of awareness and connections to other, more subtle and fleeting forms are available to us through epiphanies, synchronicities, mystical experiences, and other special moments when individual human consciousness merges into something much greater. Our minds and bodies all have access to the same creative source that animates every atom and star. The world that is created in unitary thought is only the smallest fragment of a much greater reality, for we can live and have direct awareness of a universe that is beyond all forms, images, and theories.

■ Emergence of New Structures

The Big Bang theory of the origin of the universe suggests that an initial featureless bath of energy evolved into everything from the elementary particles to astronomical structures and even the earth itself. In turn, biology contends that human consciousness is the result of a long chain of evolution that began with the first macromolecules that were able to duplicate themselves on earth.

Traditionally, the emergence of new form has been pictured in a unitary way, in terms of a slow building up of complex structures out of simpler elements. This evolution of structure is also tied to limited notions of time, for what comes earlier in time is supposed to be logically prior and structurally simpler. Within our present cosmology, everything is dated from the Big Bang, and all levels and structures evolved in the great march of time from simplicity to complexity.

But what meaning does this picture have when we realize that nature is, at every level, endlessly subtle and that atoms and elementary particles are not necessarily simpler than molecules and cells? What if no particular level is more fundamental or basic than another? If complexity already exists at every level of the universe, this would suggest that the wide variety of natural forms—from plants and animals to human thought and culture—

is not the result of a linear evolution in time but a material manifestation, or flowering, of something already inherent in the very nature and creativity of the universe.

Yet while creativity and complexity are ever present, and no one level prevails over any other, it is true that structures exist today that were not explicitly present in the distant past. How, for example, is the historical evolution of life to be pictured in a nonunitary universe?

One way of looking at this question is to recognize that with each heartbeat of the universe forms manifest or unfold and then fold back. It is possible therefore that at each instant, an individual molecule or organism is immersed in, and unfolds out of, the context of its whole environment. It is possible that in that act of creative unfolding, information about the environment plays a part in re-forming each structure. In this way, novelty could manifest itself as a constant exploration of the implications of the whole environment.

We also saw how natural forms enter into communication with each other and with their environment. In this way, vital information is constantly entering into an organism that may work in active ways. Evolution is an intelligent and cooperative adjustment to an ever-changing context. And indeed, evolution itself becomes a part of that context that is changing. In fact, the universe could really be said to indulge in a form of play, a play in which processes and structures are able to feel out the implications of fresh contexts and new levels. The manifest, material world has a tendency to cling to form, yet this clinging always occurs within a particular context. Nature at play is a constant changing of contexts and the upwelling of new forms and possibilities. This play of the universe is a subtle, gentle process, a feeling out of possibilities, for at each moment, information about new environments and contents is ingested. This allows a gentle interplay and exploration of new realities that then unfold into a material manifestation.

The process could be compared with a person awaking from a deep sleep. Indeed, that image has been explicitly used, in the context of memory, by French writer Marcel Proust. The narrator of *Swann's Way* (the first book in Proust's *Remembrance of Things Past*) drifts up out of sleep into awareness. At first, he does not even recollect where he is and, half awake, makes small movements with his arms and legs. Such a situation must be familiar to most readers: You breathe quietly, stretch a foot, and move a finger and in this way slowly become aware of your own body and of the position in which you are lying. Without ever opening your eyes, you become aware of every limb and of its orientation in the bed. And as with Proust's narrator, very slowly, your body, the day, and even the room swim into conscious awareness.

This coming to a realization of the reality of the day is done in a very gentle, exploratory way. It begins with a growing realization of the body and the context in which thoughts, memories, and perceptions begin to unfold. Each morning, as we wake from sleep, we repeat the creation of the universe. Indeed, creativity involves similar gentle explorations. Matter reaches out, communicates, and explores its environment and, in this way, decides whether to cling to form or to undergo a radical change.

The evolution of the material world is a work of art. A painting, for example, begins within the thoughts, memories, and subconscious urgings of the painter, as well as in direct response to his or her perceptions of the external world. These feelings, memories, symbols, muscular dispositions, and sensory flexings of the creative impulse flow outward into the physical expression of a brush stroke. And since each brush stroke is a manifestation of form and color within the ever-changing context of the painting, the instant it is made the whole order of the painting is changed and carried back within the artist yet again.

The birth of the painting is a continual process of unfolding and enfolding, of inward ingestion and outward manifestation. It is a play of forms and color. It is trial and error. At first, it may appear tentative, yet through its constant growth and modification, the painting moves toward a final expression. In this way, forms and new orders arise—at first in a tentative way but gradually gaining more solidity. Likewise, the universe is the constant expression of a work of art. It is pure play and creativity without any reason, goal, or motive outside the very joy of creation itself.

At last the map of the world has been freed from its old restrictions and can be redrawn and colored with freedom and creativity. It is no longer bound by fixed laws and restrictive orders, for these emerge in a natural way out of its ever-changing form. Synchronicities are true patterns of the universe, connections with underlying patterns and currents that move beyond the distinction of matter and mind. They are inscape and landscape, echoes and reflections thrown out by the timeless play of the universe.

CHAPTER SEVEN

THE CHAOTIC UNIVERSE: FRACTALS, INTELLIGENCE, AND FREEDOM

■ The New Value of Knowledge

For centuries, Western society has gloried in the wealth and power of the knowledge it has accumulated. Politicians boast that more scientists are now engaged in research than have ever lived in the whole of the past, that more scientific papers are being published, and that ever more expensive experiments are being designed. Bigger data bases are built that use faster computers. Knowledge has become a commodity; indeed, computer-based expert systems attempt to reproduce specialized human skills. The goal of society has become a graph of income, efficiency, productivity, and profits that moves ever upward. More is always better; progress is founded on the accumulation of knowledge that leads to the control and manipulation of the world.

But what if this vast plan is an illusion? Knowledge is based on perceptions of what is fixed, yet if the present is always born anew, this process can never be completed. And so we try to steer the course of our evolving future and control a creative, living nature by operating from what has ceased to be. A society dominated by the authority of knowledge will never allow more subtle and creative human functions to flower, for our whole desire for certainty and control implies that we are clinging to the past and seeking security in the realm of the known.

The nonunitary universe therefore challenges us to seek a new ethic for being in a world that acknowledges both our own inner nature and the inherent richness and intrinsic creativity of our environment. In the past, the human race lived closer to the rhythms and movements of the natural world. In his marvelous book *The Forest People*, Colin M. Turnbull describes the ways of the African Pygmies.[1] To them, the forest is good: It cares for all its creatures, and the people of the forest have no need for special prayers or ceremonial pleadings. For the Pygmies, it is sufficient to sing to the forest and make it happy. We, in our society, have left the forest, the sea, and the plains far behind, and there can be no going back to them. Yet it may still be possible to learn from nature and from our own bodies and minds. If we are to play our parts as participators within nature's everlasting dance of the universe, we must learn to respond to its rhythms.

The Birth of Order

Order and chaos are viewed as opposing forces. Order is seen in a positive light. It is associated with harmony, law, control, regularity, discipline, determinism, form, rule, rhythm, and structure, whereas chaos is disorder, misrule, contingency, randomness, chance, and lack of harmony. In society, order is the attribute of good government, proper behavior, and human happiness, whereas chaos suggests the breakdown of order, ultimately leading to riot, revolution, and lawlessness.

Yet creative individuals like artists, composers, and writers have always appreciated the need for a measure of dissonance and irregularity within rule and order. "There is no excellent beauty that hath not some strangeness in the proportion," said Francis Bacon. And the origin stories of other cultures, particularly those of the Near East, suggest that rather than chaos emerging from the breakdown of order, it is chaos that is the generative source of the universe.

In fact, chaos and simple orders are really part of a much greater spectrum of orders and ways of seeing, which, in turn, reflect something of the richness of the universe. In the past, science focused on simple, regular orders such as the motion of planets and falling bodies, but more recently, it has become possible to make some headway in discussing richness, complexity, and endless subtlety. Scientists and mathematicians have developed a new approach to complex systems that allows for infinite detail and subtlety.[2]

While this new science, called *chaos theory*, is essentially unitary and limited to discussing only certain forms of complex order, it does, however, offer a series of metaphors that can help us toward a new vision of nature. Chaos theory points to a sensitivity within nature's systems and shows us the ultimate futility of trying to control and manipulate the world in a machinelike manner.

▪ Chaos Theory

Chaos theory is one of the most exciting theoretical developments in contemporary science. It represents science's first attempt to come to terms with systems that appear so complex in their details and motions as to be beyond all description and seeks to explain turbulent rivers, shock waves from supersonic aircraft, changes in the weather, electrical activity in the brain, irregularities in a heartbeat, complex motions of small asteroids, fluctuations in the stock market and wild swings in insect populations.

Chaos theory is part of a much greater topic called *nonlinear dynamics* that goes far beyond the simple regular trajectories and phase spaces of Newtonian physics. Nonlinear dynamics deals with abrupt and catastrophic changes, random motions, infinite sensitivity, and bifurcation points (which are a sort of crossroads in the evolution of a system). It radically extends our earlier phase space picture and provides a framework for understanding how systems can generate their own internal structures and stabilities. It deals with shapes that are infinitely complex in their nature, such as river deltas, the tracery of trees, lungs, the human circulatory system, frost patterns on a window, and the pattern of fractures in a metal rod.

▓ Fractals

One of the most immediate inroads into chaos theory is by means of what are called fractals. The images produced using fractals may be familiar to many readers. They have appeared in a number of books and a host of articles in popular science magazines. As well as being fascinating mathematical objects in their own right, fractals are also able to simulate the appearance of landscapes, planets, and a variety of organic forms. Indeed, fractals are used to generate the complex shapes seen in many advertisements, films, and television commercials. Every day people are looking at fractal images without even realizing it.

Greek mathematicians explored the spatial orders of two-dimensional forms such as the line, triangle, square, and circle as well as a variety of solid figures such as the cube, sphere, and pyramid. Euclid used formal logic to analyze the properties and relationships involved in the geometry of these figures. And it was believed by Plato that ideal forms lay at the basis of nature. Such ideas persisted throughout the Renaissance, and many instruction books on drawing divided the human figure into ellipses, circles, and rectangles.

The essence of nature's structures, it was believed, can be found in a geometry that is over two thousand years old. But what about really complicated figures like trees, coastlines, mountains, and the shapes of clouds? The problem was that they appeared too messy and were simply not the sort of systems that any respectable mathematician would want to bother about. With a world of aesthetic mathematics in which to journey, who would want to concern himself or herself with accidental bumps and wiggles?

Measuring a Coastline

A few mathematicians began to wonder just how it would be possible to describe such eccentric shapes in rigorous terms. It soon looked as if a whole new set of mathematical ideas would have to be developed to take them into account. Think, for example, of the coastline of a country such as Britain, with all its details of estuaries, rocky promontories, and smooth sandy regions. Mathematicians wondered how to calculate the circumference of Britain's coastline. In the case of a football field or a table top, it is a simple matter to wrap a piece of string around it, unwind the string, then measure its length. But how can we do this with a coastline?

One could begin by taking a tourist map of the whole country. Place a piece of thread around the coast and then measure its length using the scale at the bottom of the map. This certainly appears to give the length of the British coast. But it is possible to purchase a more detailed set of road maps that divides the country into five or six regions. These maps show, for example, the estuaries of smaller rivers and large streams and do not smooth out so many details on the coastline. Repeating the measuring process with this series of maps gives a different result: The coastline turns out to be longer. And there are yet other maps; the British Ordinance Survey, for example, produces a beautiful set of over two hundred maps that give information about almost every footpath in the country. With the help of such maps, it is possible to loop the thread around every mile of the coastline and take in the effects of even more detail. But now the coastline appears to be even longer.

So where does this process end? What is the correct answer, the true length of Britain's coastline? Each time one goes to a

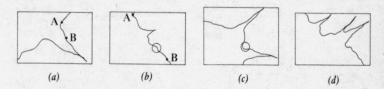

Figure 7.1. According to map (*a*), the distance between A and B is one mile. But in the larger scale map (*b*), in which more detail is shown, the distance is two and a half miles. A detail of map (*b*) is displayed in map (*c*) and an even larger-scale portion of this map is given in (*d*). In each case, with more detail, the distance between A and B increases.

more detailed map, the answer gets bigger (Figure 7.1). Perhaps you should pace out the distance on foot. And if so, should you include all the small deviations, the tiny promontories, and the estuaries of every small stream? To make a shortcut across such details is to leave out a tiny segment of the true coastline. And does this mean that even the sides of all the individual rocks along the coast should be included? And does one add in pebbles and even grains of sand?

In each case, the result becomes longer and longer—without limit. In fact, the true circumference of the British coast is the same as that of North and South America combined! It is infinite. Thanks to the infinite detail of natural forms, the circumference of the British Isles is infinitely long.

A coastline is created by a wide variety of processes. In one region, the surging sea breaks down cliffs and rocks; in another, a sea marsh dries out or sand silts up a bay. Add to this the streams and rivers that cut their way through the land and meander into the sea, add the constant action of wind, rain, and tides, and the result is a highly complex natural shape—a shape that cannot be reproduced through the simple expedient of adding a layer of detail to some underlying simpler shape.

Natural coastlines are of infinite length and endless complexity. When it comes to mountains, we discover that they have no definite slope. Viewed from a distance, a mountain may have a fairly well defined shape, but approach the mountain, and that shape begins to vary from region to region and eventually from

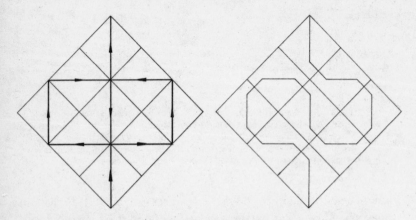

Figure 7.2. The Peano curve. In a series of steps this curve becomes progressively more complicated until it fills the entire plane. As it does so, its fractal dimension increases from 1.0 to 2.0.

place to place. In fact, the sorts of mathematical objects that define the complicated shape of a mountainside turn out to have no slope!

Of course, provided that it is not too steep, an engineer is still able to build a railway track up the mountainside with a definite length and gradient. But this is because each metal rail has a finite length and the track itself smooths out the ever-changing deviations of the mountainside. At this level, conventional geometry can be used by an engineer, yet if the details of the mountain slope were to be explored at finer and finer scales, such concepts as length and slope would begin to slip away in the face of infinite complexity (Figure 7.2).

In response to these curious discoveries about the shapes of real objects, mathematicians were challenged to reproduce such shapes themselves and began to create lines of greater and greater complexity. They devised curves with endless twists and turns, surfaces with limitless detail, lines with no slope but infinite length, and as they began to study these lines and surfaces, they discovered that the very notion of dimension was beginning to topple.

■ New Dimensions

In the world of regular Greek geometry, the idea of a dimension is cut and dried. A point has zero dimension, "location without extension," as the school geometry books put it. A line has one dimension, a plane (the surface of this piece of paper) has two dimensions, and space itself has three. We are familiar with zero, one, two, and three dimensions. But as with a coastline, mathematicians discovered that an infinitely complex and slopeless line has a dimension that is higher than unity. A coastline has a dimension that lies between that of a line and a plane. Its dimension is a fraction, and in the case of Britain's coastline, it is 1.26.

These infinitely subtle shapes and figures require a redefinition of the whole meaning of dimensions, for the old and accepted definitions simply cannot address their inner complexity. While the new definitions are quite technical, one way of imagining a fractional dimension is to think of a table top that is covered with many grains of rice. There may be a million grains on the table, but a straight line goes through only a few thousand of them. The number of grains covered by the line and by the table top are radically different. But suppose that the line becomes increasingly complex and starts to pass over more and more grains. What happens when the line touches nearly all the grains? Is the line still one-dimensional, or has it, in its complexity, begun to approach the two-dimensional plane? Highly complex lines, so complex that they have no slope and their lengths are infinite, have a fractional dimension higher than one.

Fractal mathematicians went from lines to surfaces of such complexity that their dimensions lie between two and three. They even discovered a collection of points, called a Cantor dust, whose dimension is between zero and one. Suddenly mathematics was plunged into a world of fractional dimensions and forced to admit lines that are of infinite length yet fit on a finite piece of paper as well as some continuous curves that have no slope. The word *fractal* was coined for these fractionally dimensioned objects, and their champion, Benoit Mandelbrot, claimed that fractal dusts, curves, and surfaces are really much closer to the forms of nature than anything that has hitherto been invented in mathematics.

Remember how nature was constrained to lie on the grid of Dürer and Descartes? Forcing nature to become orderly and regular was connected to the imposition of a Cartesian coordinate system and to the mathematical calculus. With the help of this calculus, Newton was able to calculate the paths of everything from cannon balls to planets. But the paths Newton and others worked with were always regular and simple; they had finite lengths and well-defined slopes. Indeed, the very prerequisite for using Newton's calculus is that slopes must be regular and well defined. What use is all this mighty mathematics now that a path no longer possesses a slope and cannot be differentiated? What if certain objects move along trajectories that are so complicated that they have a fractional dimension? Suddenly, the whole mathematical underpinning of the Newtonian worldview falls apart.

Laplace believed that if he had stood beside God at the moment of creation, he would have been able to compute the movement of every particle in the universe right until the end of time. But what if some particles take fractal paths and are involved in motions that lie beyond the capabilities of the mathematical calculus? Suddenly, the richness of nature lies far beyond the capabilities of Newton's map.

Mandelbrot is saying that all regular descriptions are an illusion and have nothing to do with the real world of clouds, mountains, stars, fast-flowing rivers, and driving rain. Such phenomena are infinitely complex and require a totally different mathematics—the mathematics of fractals.

■ Generating Fractals

Yet despite their apparent complexity, simple fractals are quite easy to generate. In fact, one can be developed out of a simple triangle by using what Mandelbrot calls a generator. In Figure

7.3, each side of the triangle is replaced by a simple shape (called the generator) to produce a star.

In the next step, the generator is scaled down by one third, and the process is repeated using each straight line in the star to produce an even more complicated shape. This can go on indefinitely, each time the generator is scaled down by one third and applied to every straight line in the figure. In this fashion, the figure grows in complexity and shows more and more detail. By applying the generator at smaller and smaller scales without limit, one ends up with a fractal—a figure having no slope and an infinite circumference. Moreover, one can see by its very generation how its detail repeats over and over again. Take any small part of the fractal and magnify it; more detail will be seen. Now magnify a tiny part of that figure, and even more detail is discovered. In each case, the detail repeats. As mathematicians put it, it is self-similar.

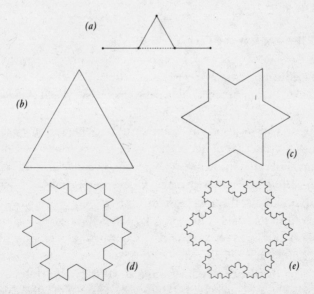

Figure 7.3. Applying a generator (*a*) to a triangle (*b*) results in a six-sided star (*c*). Progressive applications of the generator, each time being scaled down by a factor of 1/3, results in ever more complex figures (*d*), (*e*). In the limit a fractal figure is obtained.

A wide variety of quite different looking fractals can be generated in this way, all showing endless complexity and detail. These include fractal islands, fractal mountains, and even fractal dusts. There are fractals that show endless branching and simulate the shapes of river deltas, trees, lungs, and the nervous system. There are fractals that pertain to clouds or to the convolutions of the brain.

Some fractals show strict self-similarity; that is, they have the same detail that repeats at each level of scale. Others show variations in detail at different scales, and some are termed *random fractals*. According to fractal mathematicians, these fractals can model such things as blood circulation systems, electronic noise, the distribution of stars and galaxies in the universe, turbulence, metal fractures, frost on a window pane, shock waves from a supersonic aircraft, the nasal bones of an Arctic fox, polymers, the electronic signals from the brain, and irregularities in a human heartbeat.

■ The Mandelbrot Set

One of the most widely researched of fractals is called the *Mandelbrot set*. A number of computer programs have been developed that allow one to "fly into" the Mandelbrot set on a personal computer and so display its complexities. (Some of these can be obtained within the public domain.) The set has been called the most complicated mathematical object in the universe, and again, it shows limitless and varied detail. One can zoom in to a particular tiny piece of detail and explore its inner structure at higher and higher magnifications. Indeed, the Mandelbrot set is a whole universe in miniature, for one can go on and on, exploring all its implications and details without end.

What is particularly interesting about the Mandelbrot set is that it was not so much created by a mathematician as discovered. This curious mathematical object depends directly on the properties of what are called *complex numbers*. All one needs to do in order to generate the Mandelbrot set is to select a complex number and endlessly iterate it back into itself. In this sense, therefore, the Mandelbrot set was always present and waiting within the properties of the complex numbers for some mathematician to stumble upon it. No one really invented the Mandelbrot set—mathematicians simply came across it in all its endless complexity.

Earlier we saw how we can enter the universe at any level and explore it through all its endless detail. The Mandelbrot set gives a metaphor for this interior complexity of all things, for the more you "fly" your computer into the set, the more it opens out to receive you. There is no end to the Mandelbrot set, and to fly inside is to participate in the unfolding of a mathematical symphony. In a similar fashion, one can enter any level of nature and be faced with endless detail.

But there is an irony to this so-called most complex object in the universe: It is generated in a particularly simple way, by a simple act of iteration. One takes the output from one stage of the interaction and feeds it back as input for the next stage. In all its complexity, the Mandelbrot set is being unfolded in a mechanical way. Indeed, all fractals are generated by a simple act of repetition or iteration, so that they are at one and the same time both highly complex and yet ordered in a very simple way.

▨ Trees and Fractals

Does this mean that it is simply fortuitous that fractals appear to mimic the complexity found in coastlines and clouds, lungs, rivers, and trees? Think of all the constraints and contingencies that operate on a single tree growing in the woods. The tree grows and survives by the processes of photosynthesis that occur in its leaves. It possesses a leaf-supporting structure that offers a maximum surface area to the sun. But the sun does not lie in one fixed position in the sky; it moves from east to west, and its maximum altitude differs with the seasons. Moreover, nearby trees or buildings may cut off light at certain times of the day.

And having maximum leaf surface area is not enough. The tree must be constructed so that its trunk can support all that weight without breaking; this requires that branches and twigs grow in a certain way and that the ratio of their diameters to that of the trunk is of a certain order. In addition, the tree must be able to withstand high winds. It must be able to drain off an excess of water from its foliage during heavy rain and allow for some of that water to reach the ground near its roots. If a tree grows on the side of a mountain or on a coast, it may have to contend with a prevailing wind. Moreover, all these various restrictions on the design of the tree happen to apply at one point in time—but in fact, the tree itself must grow from a seedling, developing branches as it grows. It may begin life in the shadow of other trees or in an open field, and for each year of its growth, a variety of external constraints may apply to its shape, to its rate of growth, and to the decision as to where branches will form and how much foliage will grow. Each of these design decisions is then carried within the structure and form of the growing tree as it moves toward maturity.

A fractal design goes some way to explaining the complex branching of a tree. Certain fractals do indeed have the appearance of trees, and by modifying the simple rule by which the fractal is generated, it is possible to generate different generic shapes for oak, poplar, and evergreen. But a real living tree is like a book: It is the manifestation of forces and decisions that were made within its lifetime. From the first seedling to the gnarled and cracked trunk of an ancient oak, the tree speaks to us of its life, the variations in the seasons it has experienced, times of drought and low temperatures, changes in the vegetation around it, and even the birds and animals that have been sheltered in its body. A tree is a unique individual, and as every artist and every Native person knows, it has a spirit.

While fractals are able to reproduce the generic branching form of a tree, they only represent an ideal tree, a tree dedicated to perfection. The fractal tree stands to the particular living tree in a forest as does the "Venus de Milo" to an individual living woman. Of course, it is possible to allow for a random element at some of its branchings and so give the appearance of contingency and individuality in growth. But does the fractal really capture the *essence* of a real tree's individual shape? While the aspects of its branching are produced mathematically, does not something always escape? Is nature really that simple?

Fractals give powerful new insights into the nature of complexity, but they are not the final and true representations of the inherent organic subtlety of nature. Fractals are generated according to a relatively simple procedure. By contrast, the living structures of nature are generated in a far more subtle fashion, for their very existence depends on a much wider and ever-changing context.

■ Algorithms and Intelligence

The processes of iteration whereby fractals are generated are also called *algorithms*. Algorithms involve a process or calculation that uses a small number of simple steps repeated over and over again, the output of one complete cycle being fed back as the input of the next. Algorithms go far beyond the production of fractal shapes; they can be used to mimic a variety of processes. Some scientists believe that they mirror the generative processes used by nature.

In his book *The Dreams of Reason*, the late Heinz R. Pagels argued that simple repetitive processes, or algorithms, have something in common with the basic operations of nature.[3] In Pagels's opinion, even the working of the human brain can be explained in terms of well-defined sets of algorithms. It is not so much that the shapes and structures generated by algorithms mimic those of nature but that similar iterative processes actually lie at the heart of many natural systems. This means that in principle, at least, these processes can all be simulated quite easily on a computer, for even the most complex of human and animal behaviors arise out of the repetition of very simple algorithms.

As generative processes, algorithms are unitary in nature, totally deterministic, and precisely conditioned by what went before. So while such processes may provide useful signposts to complexity, they can never, despite what Pagels claimed, reveal the true subtlety of nature. Algorithmic maps of nature provide useful signposts yet lack inner richness and authenticity.

This idea of being able to simulate human mental behavior has been the dream of the founders of artificial intelligence (AI). Many AI researchers still believe that a set of cognitive strategies underlie everything the mind does, from problem solving or recognizing a face to understanding a language and playing baseball. It is certainly true that computers have been able to mimic certain forms of human behavior. They are good at processing certain sorts of visual data and at playing chess. But their ability to understand language with all its richness and ambiguity is far from impressive. In addition, AI has not really been able to duplicate the deeper levels of human perception, with its ability to recognize and understand the visual world.

Throughout its history, artificial intelligence has suffered from a series of overoptimistic predictions that have simply failed to materialize. The most recent of these have been the dreams of the Japanese fifth-generation computer project, which proposed to develop "intelligent" computers capable of duplicating many of the functions of the human mind. The difficulties involved are far more profound than anyone expected, and the more interesting goals of this Japanese project have not been reached.

Simply because certain human behaviors can be captured in a series of cognitive algorithms, or simulated by computer, does not mean that the essence of how the human mind works and its actual generative processes have been discovered. What it really implies is that within a certain limited context it is possible to mimic certain human functions by means of a repetitive series of steps.

Again, we see another illustration of the unitary within the nonunitary. Every living moment is generated out of an inherently nonunitary process, yet within that moment there will always be an element of clinging. Unitary processes do form a large part of our mental life, for much of what we say and do has a relatively mechanical origin. In this sense, artificial intelligence, cognitive strategies, and algorithms capture the unitary aspects of human thought and behavior.

But the mind also has the capacity for endless creativity, and its functions are infinitely subtle. While certain forms of behavior may be relatively algorithmic, the mind's creativity enters through understanding the context in which this behavior is appropriate. Human insight lies in being able to transcend contexts. Computers, by contrast, are always context dependent. They are programmed to execute certain tasks in a relatively "mindless" way, and even when the context changes, the computer continues in its old way.

Of course, it is possible to add a higher-level program that instructs the computer to alter its strategies when a particular context changes. But this program itself is determined from within a more general context, and when the context of *this context* changes, the computer is unable to respond in an appropriate way. There are also programs that are supposed to learn, but this is always according to fixed strategies revolving around interpreting terms such as *success*, *goal*, or *reward*. Programs may be designed to perceive new patterns. But in all cases, the computer's behavior is fixed within some wider pattern or context.

Computers are exclusively unitary beasts; they always have boundaries and limits. By contrast, the mind is not limited by any context or plan and can always transcend the limits in which it is placed. The mind can indulge in play for play's sake; it can make a joke. It can question the context in which it finds itself and transcend its own rules. Of course, a mind that has been hurt or damaged may seek security in certain patterns of neurotic behavior, and such clinging to the past does indeed involve what could be described as unitary, algorithmic, and repetitive responses. Nevertheless, even the sickest individuals may sometimes question what they are doing and gain the insight that allows them to transcend their previous limitations.

Insight, creativity, and the ability to transcend contexts are missing in artificial intelligence. Indeed, a more enlightened approach to the AI program is not to attempt to *simulate* human behavior at all but rather to attempt to extend the ability of computers to do better the things they already do well. In this way, the goal of AI would be for a computer to act as an assistant or colleague to human beings. The result would be a sort of symbiosis in which human intelligence and silicon computing power would each supplement the other's skills.

Pagels's claim that everything in nature from complex material processes to the human mind can be seen as a series of underlying algorithms must be rejected. Algorithms are mechanical, unitary, and deterministic—nature is not. And while the endless repetition of a particular algorithm by a high-speed computer can produce shapes of staggering complexity, this is not a duplication of the essential processes of nature.

So while fractals provide our first vision of endless complexity and detail, they do not give us the final word. At best, the fractal provides an antidote to earlier and more simplistic descriptions of nature. And just as we were once caught in the grip of the ideal forms of Greek geometry, we should now take care not to be mesmerized by the apparent power of fractals.

■ Pendulums

Fractals open a door to the endless complexity of nature. The examples given above focused on static forms rather than on dynamic processes and change, but with the help of fractals, it is possible to enter the world of chaotic motion, turbulence, and infinitely complex movements. In order to do this, we will revitalize and deepen the phase map that we left behind several chapters ago. This new phase space will be rich with structure and information.

As a first step toward enriching the phase space picture, think of the pendulum of a clock. In an ideal world, in which there is

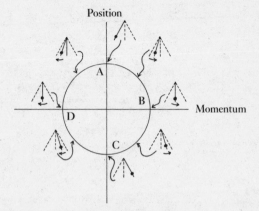

Figure 7.4. A phase space diagram for a pendulum. At the top of its swing, *A*, the pendulum is at its maximum displacement from its midpoint and has zero velocity. At the midpoint *B* the pendulum has maximum speed but zero displacement. Note that while it has the same speed at *D* it is moving in the opposite direction and therefore its momentum is different.

no friction or air resistance, a pendulum swings back and forth in a constant way—swinging first to the right and then to the left. As it reaches the top of its swing to the left, it slows down, and for an infinitesimal fraction of a second, it stops, then reverses its motion and begins to speed up again as its center of gravity falls. In the middle of the swing, it is moving at its fastest speed, but then, as it climbs to the right, it begins to slow down again. And so the pendulum oscillates—increasing and decreasing its speed, first approaching, then moving away from its midpoint.

It is easy to draw the swing of a pendulum in phase space (Figure 7.4). The pendulum moves between extremes of velocity, for as it reaches its midpoint with successive swings, it is traveling at the same speed but in the opposite direction, that is, with an opposite velocity. At the highest points to the left and right, its velocity is zero. In addition, the pendulum also swings between extremes of distance from its midpoint. Figure 7.5 shows that when its velocity is zero, its distance from the midpoint is maximum—it is at the top of its swing. And when it is at its midpoint (zero displacement), its velocity is maximum.

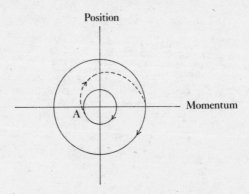

Figure 7.5. A pendulum is given a small push, at A, which causes it to swing faster and farther. Its phase space diagram spirals outward and settles down in a new cycle.

Left to itself, the phase space point that represents this ideal pendulum will circle endlessly in phase space. Its back and forth swing in real space is pictured as a circular oscillation in phase space.

Give the pendulum a small push at exactly the right moment and it will speed up, describing a slightly larger circle (Figure 7.5). Conversely, if we allow for the influence of the air, the pendulum will experience air resistance as it swings back and forth; with each swing, it will be slowed down a little, and consequently, it will not be able to reach as high as it did on the previous swing. The effect of air resistance is to cut down the extremes of velocity and position for the pendulum, and the result is to cause the point in phase space to spiral inward to a final resting place—a pendulum that swings no more.

An ideal pendulum is not stable. An extra push will force its phase space point to move in a wider circle, whereas air resistance will cause it to spiral inward. But a pendulum in a clock does not do this. It receives a periodic kick—exactly timed by its own swing—to compensate for the effects of friction and air resistance. When this small periodic driving force is added to the pendulum, it causes it to perform a constant circular motion in

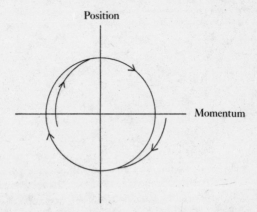

Figure 7.6. In the case of a limit cycle, the pendulum's motion is stable. Given a small push, the pendulum will always be attracted back to its limit cycle motion.

phase space. If the pendulum is given a tiny push to knock it off course, it will quickly return to its original path in phase space. Try to slow it down, and it will speed up again. Even air resistance has no effect on its motion.

Limit Cycles

Such a pendulum is dynamically stable, for it resists the effects of tiny pushes, knocks, and air resistance, always returning to its stable motion. Its circular path in phase space is termed a *limit cycle*, for it represents the final goal to which the pendulum returns after it has been perturbed or interfered with (Figure 7.6). It is almost as if this limit cycle exercised a sort of magnetic attraction for the point in phase space.

Limit cycles are not confined to clocks—in fact, they abound in nature. What could be more different than a fish and a clock, yet both can become involved in cyclic behavior! Think of a lake that contains both trout and pike. If in one year the number of trout happens to fall, then the pike will lose some of their food supply and begin to die out. With a smaller number of pike to prey on them, the remaining trout have a higher chance of survival

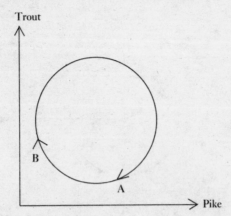

Trout

B

A

Pike

Figure 7.7. Limit cycles characterize many natural systems. Here pike and trout become locked into a limit cycle. For when the number of trout falls too low (A), the pike are starved of their prey and begin to die out. With fewer pike (B), the number of trout can increase.

and increase their population. As the number of trout grows, so does the food supply of the pike, which increase in number and, in the process, reduce the trout population yet again. So year after year, decade after decade, the population of pike and trout chase each other around their limit cycles (Figure 7.7). This sort of behavior is characteristic of the relationships that exist between many predators and their prey. The remarkable thing about such

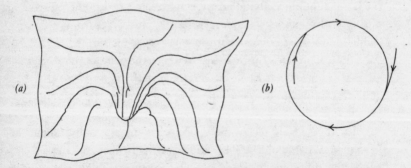

(a)

(b)

Figure 7.8. Many of nature's systems can be pictured as moving through a richly landscaped phase space with mountains, valleys, saddle points, and plains. Here a phase space mountain is surrounded by a deep circular valley (a). The phase space point corresponding to a system will run around the valley floor. The result is a limit cycle (b), for whenever the system is displaced up the mountain it rolls back into the valley floor again.

systems is their dynamic stability: If you perturb the system a little, it always bounces back to its original behavior. Throw in a few extra pike or a few extra trout one year, and the same limit cycle soon reestablishes itself.

It is as if the phase space in which the system moves is no longer a flat space but a rich landscape, and the system is a ball rolling through that landscape. In the case of a limit cycle, the phase space landscape takes the form of a circular canal between two sets of mountains (Figure 7.8). The ball, which represents the pendulum's motion in phase space, or the populations of pike and trout, rolls endlessly along the bottom of the canal, and every time it is displaced—by pushing it up the side of the mountain—it falls back toward the canal again. For obvious reasons, this canal is called an *attractor*.

Whenever the various parts of a system work together collectively to produce stability or repetitive motion, then somewhere within the rich geography of phase an attractor is to be found. This landscape can be quite complicated, with mountain ranges, ridges, and different sorts of valleys. The simplest of these is the symmetric attractor basin, one of which is illustrated in Figure 7.9. In this case, a disturbed system always falls back to

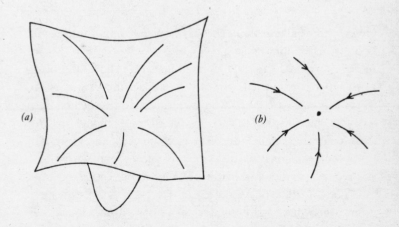

Figure 7.9. In this case the landscape contains an attractor basin (*a*). When perturbed, the system always returns to its same limit point (*b*).

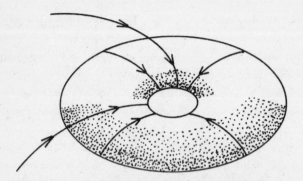

Figure 7.10. The phase space of a natural system will have very many dimensions. In figure 7.8 a circular valley in three dimensions causes the system to be locked into a limit cycle. However, in this case a four-dimensional generalization of this valley (not shown) causes the phase space point to be attracted to the surface of a torus.

the bottom of the valley—to a *limit point*. Attractors having other geometries may cause the phase space point to move on a limit cycle or even to wind around the surface of a donut, as shown in Figure 7.10.

▓ Spontaneous Structure and Phase Space Landscapes

One way of thinking about chaos theory and nonlinear dynamics is in terms of the landscape of phase space. Stability, chaos, bifurcation points, and catastrophic change are all features of this phase space landscape. Enriching phase space in this way evokes something of the richness of the maps discussed in the first chapter. The older maps of science are not powerful enough to direct us through these new landscapes of complexity and sensitivity. We must tread softly as we enter this new and uncharted land, and we will require a new way of being and of acting.

The idea that phase space can develop a rich landscape of its own goes back to those cases of self-organization that were discussed in earlier chapters, for whenever a system develops cooperative behavior, this is reflected in the landscape of phase space. The phase space of Chapter 1 was a simple, regular, flat geometry, but the more the internal variables of a system lock together and intertwine, the richer becomes the geometry of phase space and the more complex is our journey through it. The living systems of nature demand a phase space of equal richness and compel us to devise new maps for our journeys through the natural world.

A wide variety of natural systems spontaneously develop their own stabilities. Our bodies preserve the same internal temperature in winter or summer. When the weather is too cold, our metabolism speeds up to maintain this body temperature. When it is too hot, we perspire. Other systems maintain the correct level of oxygen and glucose in the brain, balance electrolytes, adjust blood pressure, and so on.

But stability is not simply the province of living systems. The astronomical number of electrons in a superconductor work in harmony to guide individual electrons around obstructions so that they do not scatter and give rise to turbulence in the overall flow of the electron gas. In the case of the superconductor, it is the overall collective form of the wave function, and the structure of Hilbert space, that maintains the stable flow of an electrical current. And this is but one example from a host of other systems in physics, chemistry, and biology.

Dynamic stability, which emerges out of the whole internal order of a system, is very different from the inert stability of a rock that simply sits on a mountain top. It operates in an active way to resist external change and, when finally disturbed, acts to return the system to its original behavior. Dynamic stability can also apply to development. Biologist Conrad Hall Waddington provided the image of a developing organism as a ball that rolls down a gully on a hillside.[4] In the case of an attractor, if we interfere with the ball and divert it from its path in phase space, it will soon regain its stabile motion (Figure 7.11). But, Waddington pointed out, a growing organism does even more than this: If the ball is pushed off its path, it does not return to the location it occupied *before* it was disturbed. Rather, it moves for-

Figure 7.11. Conrad Waddington pictured a developing organism as a ball that rolls downhill in a river valley. But this valley plays an even more powerful role than a normal phase space attractor, for when the organism is displaced from its normal development, it not only returns to the valley but catches up to the position it would have been occupying if left undisturbed (homeorhesis).

ward, to where it would have been if no disturbance had acted in the first place! While homeostasis is the ability of a system to return to a state of stable equilibrium—like a constant body temperature or blood pressure—*homeorhesis* is the power of a growing organism to remain on track in its development, so that when it has been artificially retarded, it is still able to catch up with its developmental schedule.

To Waddington, living systems are self-correcting. They carry within themselves an active map of their landscape, with its hills and valleys, mountain peaks, and saddles so that if these systems are ever perturbed out of their normal path, they are able to find their way back again and arrive on schedule. The maps that are held by nature's systems are active and dynamic, they depend on contexts, and they are replete with meaning.

■ A Landscape of Life

Waddington's idea of a landscape of life can be taken even further in this book. We have seen how systems can communicate with each other at the quantum level and how a quantum system can "feel out" its environment. Collective quantum oscillations within a biological system, for example, give rise to long-range signals. And like the echo sounding system in a bat, these signals are modulated by the surrounding environment and may be picked up again to give information about what lies outside a cell or organism. A living system was also pictured as moving within a great electromagnetic ocean, and an ocean of sound waves, smells, and mechanical vibrations.

Life responds to this vast, active, and ever-changing landscape of information. Waddington as well as nonlinear scientists have pictured this landscape as being richly structured, with attractor basins and valleys, high mountains, peaks, saddles, and passes. Another landscape would be a holographic or, to use David Bohm's term, an implicate, or enfolded, order.

An implicate order is best explained in terms of a holograph. The first holographs were made so that information about the entire scene was enfolded within every part of the holographic plate. Or, to use Bohm's language, the explicate forms within the scene were transformed into the implicate order of the holographic image. Break off a piece of a normal photograph, and you capture only part of the scene, but every fragment of a holographic plate contains information about the entire scene.

The idea of an implicate, or holographic, order connects to the ideas of nonlocality that were briefly discussed with reference to Bell's theorem. John Bell showed that distant quantum objects remain actively correlated without the need for some intermediary field or mechanical connection. One way this could be pictured is for quantum forms to unfold out of a deeper implicate order. Two electrons would therefore be in contact at the implicate level but well separated at the explicate level.

Suppose that life itself moves within a field of enfolded information, something that is partly analogous to a holograph. In this way, it is possible to respond to distant processes and, at every point, to have access to a wide field of information. In turn, it may be possible to feed back one's response and thereby transform that holographic field of information.

Indeed, if the human mind and body could enter into direct communion with this ocean of active information, it would have access to forms and patterns that transcend the boundaries between inner and outer, mind and matter—in other words, to synchronicities. The Chinese sages had their own account of the synchronicities of the I Ching. Our manifest world is, they said, the reflection of a much deeper reality that lies outside the domain of time. Synchronicities are embryonic moments that contain the enfolded potentialities of this transcendent reality. Through contemplations of the patterns that can be discerned within these special moments, it becomes possible to unfold the potentialities of the manifest universe. Likewise, to see the universe as a vast ocean of information suggests that we can grasp within it particular images that contain hints of the transcendent unfolding of the universe.

The idea that each living being is an active participant in an ocean of information also has important implications for the human body and its immune system. In an earlier chapter, we saw how quantum structures express their collective nature by crystallizing out of an underlying sea of ambiguity. In turn, a quantum system can enter into active communication with other molecules in its environment. A particular molecular structure or process could therefore be thought of as the material manifestation of a web of information and exchange. Likewise, the information within this ocean is a manifestation of the vibrations and reactions of material forms. Active information and material processes become two sides, or aspects, of a single whole.

The Immune System

The human immune system, for example, could be thought of both as a dynamic pattern of molecular flows and processes and as a harmonious pattern of meaning that dances through the body. The immune system is both a material process and a sort of corporate intelligence of the whole body. Indeed, there are parallels between the immune system and the human brain and nervous system. Both are of a comparable complexity; in fact, certain neurotransmitters (brain chemicals responsible for the transmission of information) respond to receptors within the immune system. Just as one aspect of the human brain lies in its ability to recognize patterns, so does the immune system recognize the patterns of foreign proteins and other harmful substances.

The immune system is the body's dialogue and thinking center. It could be compared with a group of hunters that sit around a fire late at night to exchange stories, sing songs, and talk about the events of the day. This dialogue restores harmony to the group and gives rise to a corporate meaning that reanimates values and reaffirms each person's role. Likewise, the dialogue of the immune system operates at every level within the body and so is like a fractal in that it works at an infinity of levels, from processes within the cell to individual organs to general regulation of metabolism. It is enfolded at the molecular level, as metabolic regulations and nerve impulses, and in the body's larger-scale patterns and flows. Through this active dialogue, the body works to maintain a dynamic harmony and to resist the challenges of harmful substances—like trauma, foreign proteins—from outside.

A dialogue of active information also embraces the whole of society, for when a group is bound together through a cohesive meaning, they are able to respond to the challenges of change. Indeed, the values and meanings of a society become a collective immune system. And just as the human body becomes ill when—through some harmful agent in the environment or a breakdown in its own meaning—it ceases to act coherently, so, too, society can fragment into violent and meaningless activity.

◼ Strange Attractors

The complex landscape of a nonlinear system contains a variety of attractors such as basins and valleys, geographical formations

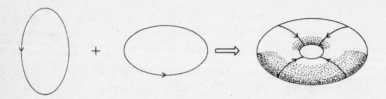

Figure 7.12. Two limit cycles combine to form a donut, or torus attractor. The phase space point now winds around the surface of the donut. Donuts can themselves combine to form yet higher dimensional tori.

that stabilize the system and cause it to resist change. But there is yet another sort of attractor, called a strange attractor, that represents the marriage between phase space and fractals. This strange attractor lies at the heart of chaos theory.

Think of a flowing river. In the summer, when the water level is low and the river flows slowly, its surface is very smooth. As you drift along with the current in a small boat, tiny specks in the water drift along beside you at exactly the same speed— never moving away from the boat, never rushing past it. In this case, the motion of the water would be represented by a *limit point*, for the velocity of the water does not change and small specks in the water do not vary their separation from each other. The corresponding attractor would be a basin. Whenever it is disturbed by throwing in a rock, the flow of the river always returns to the same limit point (constant velocity and unchanging separation between all its regions).

Following heavy rain, the river speeds up and vortices begin to form. These are quite stable in themselves; even the act of throwing a stone into the water will not disturb them for long. Such vortices are represented by limit cycles.

Finally, in spring, with the water running even faster, new smaller vortices form within the bigger vortices. The speed of the water varies more rapidly from place to place, specks in the river rapidly swing away from each other, and the motion must be represented by a phase space point that spirals around a donut. (This donut could be thought of as the superposition of two limit cycles, as shown in Figure 7.12.)

And what happens if the river speeds up even more? The result is turbulence, a highly complex disturbance of the water, which Leonardo da Vinci pictured as containing vortices within vortices within vortices.

How is this additional complexity to be pictured in terms of attractor geometries? At one time, physicists believed that it was simply a matter of using attractors of greater and greater complexity, that is, populating the phase space landscape with ever more complicated forms. For example, since a vortex within a vortex is represented by a point that spirals around a donut—that is, that moves on the two-dimensional surface of a three-dimensional object—the next stage of complexity would be a sort of superdonut, involving movement on the three-dimensional surface of a four-dimensional object! And why stop there? Why not keep extending the dimensions of phase space till we have movement on the five-dimensional surface of a six-dimensional donut, and so on? Such generalizations would begin to explain the levels of detail within detail within detail that are to be found in a turbulent river.

Not so, it turns out. The answer, it appears, is not to extend the geometry of attractors and limit cycles to higher and higher dimensions. Rather, it is to move from the conventional geometry of well-defined dimensions to that of fractals. Physicists now believe that as the speed of a river increases, the attractor suddenly jumps from being the regular, well-behaved surface of a donut to a fractal.

In other words, the surface of the donut stops being a regular, well-behaved geometrical figure and explodes into limitless detail. The result is what physicists and mathematicians call a *strange attractor*. It is called "strange" because it has no regular geometry. A strange attractor occupies a finite region of phase space, yet its surface area is infinite, its surface has no slope, and as a mathematical function, it cannot be differentiated because its detail is endless.

If the speed and position of an object are determined by the way it moves from place to place in phase space on the surface of its attractor, just think how bizarre that motion becomes when the attractor's surface is a fractal! The object's velocity may, for example, swing wildly, first moving this way and then that. Two tiny neighboring specks in the river may suddenly find themselves a great distance apart from each other or even swing back together.

In fact, this is exactly what one expects to see in a turbulent river, and the idea that the motion of the river is linked to a strange attractor—a fractal—seems intuitively correct. In a turbulent river, things do vary erratically from place to place, the river's flow seems totally chaotic, and it appears to show no discernible order, for now the endless details of fractals have been translated into the infinite complexity of the river's flow. And strange attractors apply to far more than rivers; they also characterize such diverse things as the shock wave from a supersonic aircraft, a thunderstorm, and sudden wild swings in the stock market.

Sensitivity

An important aspect of a chaotic system is its extreme sensitivity. Think, for example, of a multilane expressway. In the middle of the day, traffic flows in a smooth fashion and a driver can easily become locked into moving at the same uniform speed as the rest of the traffic. Two cars that enter the highway at the same point will tend to remain close to each other because the traffic itself acts as an attractor. But things are different during the rush hour: Lanes move at different speeds; some become blocked; others move ahead in bursts. Get into the wrong lane and you may find yourself barely creeping along for the next half hour, whereas a lane change may get you past a traffic block and moving at speed, only to become trapped a mile or two later. The problem is that the motion of your car depends very sensitively on what all the other cars around you are doing, and they in turn depend on what yet other cars, including your own, are doing. It is the exact reverse of the smooth, cooperative behavior that occurs in the superconductor in which the large population of electrons behave cooperatively to ensure a smooth flow.

Systems that are dominated by chaotic attractors, like rush-hour traffic and turbulent rivers, share several things in common. They have an incredibly complex and chaotic motion in which it is really no longer a practical possibility to predict how any one part of the system will behave. Nearby regions do not stay together but can rapidly diverge in their velocities and their distance of separation. They are so sensitive that the slightest interference may push part of the system in some radically new direction.

The behavior of such chaotic and complex systems is far from the simple regularities that were once treated by science. Nature is beginning to display its irrational side, for the point about chaos is that it sets a limit on how humans can predict and control the natural world. The ethical and practical implications of these limits will be unfolded in the next chapter. But at least we now begin to see the extent to which systems can become internally sensitive and interdependent, so that whatever happens within one region depends critically on what is going on in every other. This interdependence is clearly of key importance when we come to consider issues such as ecology, social order, and global politics.

Chaotic Bugs

Strange attractors are just one of several ways of entering into the infinite complexity of nature. Another approach is to study the way insect populations fluctuate from year to year.

Sitting on a patio in the late evening, you speculate on the large number of bugs that summer and assume that it is because of a particularly mild winter or an unusually wet spring. It comes as a great surprise to learn that sudden fluctuations in insect populations need not be related to an external cause but can arise from within the complex internal dynamics of the insect population itself. The numbers of insects in your garden can range from long-term stability, through yearly oscillations, right up to chaos.

For simplicity, imagine an insect that lives through the summer, lays its eggs in the fall, and then dies. In the following year, these eggs hatch and we get a new population of insects. If the egg-laying rate per insect is low, the bugs will eventually die out; but if it is high, we can expect to get more and more insects each year. If, for example, there are B eggs laid for every bug, B becomes a sort of birthrate. The equation for population reads:

$$\text{Population}_{(this\ year)} = B \times \text{Population}_{(last\ year)}.$$

When B is equal to 1, there is one bug born for every bug that dies, and the population is totally stable. If B is less than 1, the bugs will eventually die out; on the other hand, if B is greater than 1, they will increase without limit.

The problem with an ever-expanding insect population is that if it goes on unchecked, there will be bugs everywhere, and nowhere left for us humans to sit! But this does not happen because insects have natural enemies such as birds, frogs, and bats, and moreover, if there are too many insects around, their food supply will be depleted and they will die.

Clearly, a correction is needed in our equation, one that takes into account the natural tendency of populations to become limited by the territory they live in. In order to make this new equation simple, it is a good idea to redefine the way we measure a population. A bug population can be counted in thousands, tens of thousands, or even millions, but to make the arithmetic nice and easy, let us reduce everything to the same factor. Let the way we count the bug population vary between 0 and 1. Of course, the value of 1 does not mean that there is only one bug in the garden but, rather, that this is the maximum possible population that can fit into a given area. A value of 1 indicates one hundred percent population—total saturation of the area.

Similarly, a value of 0.5 will be half this maximum population—fifty percent of saturation; and 0.25 will be one quarter of this. A value of 1 may mean a thousand or a million bugs in the garden. It does not really matter.

With this new way of measuring population, let us take the absolutely easiest way of modifying our original population equation. What we need is some way of limiting the population as the area approaches saturation, that is, a population close to 1. The simplest possible factor that will pull back this population from total saturation is: $[1 - \text{Population}_{(\text{last year})}]$.

Adding on this factor, we get a new equation:

$$\text{Population}_{(\text{this year})} = B \times \text{Population}_{(\text{last year})} \times [1 - \text{Population}_{(\text{last year})}].$$

There are now the two factors in the equation involving $\text{Population}_{(\text{last year})}$, and technically speaking, this is what mathematicians call a nonlinear equation. Moreover, these two factors tend to work against each other. For example, the bigger the first expression happens to be, the more effect it has on increasing this year's population. On the other hand, the second term decreases population!

Let us see how this works in greater detail. Suppose that the insect population starts off very small, only a tiny fraction of its maximum, say, 0.05. The expression in the square brackets is 0.95, which is close to 1, and to simplify things, we may as well treat it as 1—so our equation now reads:

$$\text{Population}_{(\text{this year})} = B \times \text{Population}_{(\text{last year})} \times 1.$$

The result, as before, is an expanding population, the speed of this expansion depending on the value of B. Left to itself, this population will soon approach its maximum value of 1.

Suppose we now go to the other extreme where the population comes very close to this maximum value, say, 0.99. This time the first term (Population$_{\text{(last year)}}$) is very close to 1, so we can simply approximate it to 1 and rewrite the equation:

$$\text{Population}_{\text{(this year)}} = B \times 1 \times [1 - \text{Population}_{\text{(last year)}}].$$

The term in the square bracket is now very small. With a population of 0.99, it will be only 0.01. This very small term on the right has the effect of reducing next year's population and making it small.

In other words, the general population equation contains two factors—one that makes the population grow when it is small and the other that reduces it when it is too large (Figure 7.13). Combining the two together produces a tension between two effects, and at first sight, one would expect the result to be a sort of oscillation. And indeed this is what happens—but only for certain values of B.

Let us start with a modest birthrate of 1.5 and a small population. Year after year, the population begins to rise [Figure 7.13(a)] but not without limit, for the term in the square brackets eventually causes it to pull back if it gets too big. In fact, the population actually levels off at 0.66, two thirds of total saturation for that area; from then on, the population does not vary from year to year.

Now look what happens in the case of a birthrate of 2.5. [Figure 7.13(b)]. In this case, the population again increases but now goes through a small oscillation before it settles down at two thirds.

With the birthrate of 2.99, the population begins to oscillate in a stable way from year to year [Figure 7.13(c)]. One year there are many bugs; the next there are few. This effect has nothing to do with periodic changes in the climate or the fact that some years you forgot to spray the garden with insecticide. The oscillation arises very naturally out of the dynamics of the insect population itself.

Now look what happens when the birthrate rises even higher, to 3.0. Suddenly, we discover that the population begins a double

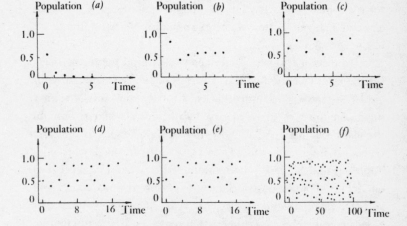

Figure 7.13. The population of insects in a finite area can vary depending on the birth rate from year to year: (a) with a birth rate of less than 1, the population soon dies out. (b) with a birthrate of 2.5, the population settles down to an equilibrium value that represents 2/3 of maximum saturation of that area. (c) with birth rate of 3.1, the population oscillates around two values, being larger in alternate years. (d) (e) with even greater birth rates, the population oscillates around 4, then 8, then 16, 32 . . . different values. (f) Finally, with a birthrate of 4.0, the population is totally chaotic.

oscillation [Figure 7.13(d)]. The value of the original population returns not every other year but once every four years. In fact, two cycles are present. At first, there is a low population; next year, a high one; the third year, a lower population (lower than in the first year); then a higher population (but not as high as in the second year). Finally, in the fourth year, we are back to the original population again. With a fixed birthrate of 3.0, such a double cycle will continue indefinitely.

Move to an increased birthrate of 3.4495, and we discover another form of behavior, a fourfold cycle in which the original insect population repeats every eight years [Figure 7.13(e)]. Increase the birthrate a little more to 3.56, and we get repetition every sixteen years; then at 3.596, every thirty-two years. From now on, very small increases in the birthrate have the effect of doubling the number of cycles in the population. Soon the fluctuation is such that over the course of a person's lifetime the number of bugs in the garden would be different every year, yet for that person's descendants, the population would repeat itself exactly. (Of course, this is with the assumption that nothing else in the garden changes.)

Even by leaving out such factors as a mild winter or a wet spring or an increased number of frogs or house martins in your garden—that is, with everything else totally constant—the very internal population dynamic itself can push the fluctuations in the insect population in a totally bizarre way. When the birthrate reaches 3.56999, the number of these different cycles becomes infinite [Figure 7.13(f)]. This means that one could collect data on the bug population for centuries on centuries and still be no closer to being able to predict next year's population. In fact, at a certain point, this cyclic fluctuation goes even beyond an infinite number of cycles and becomes entirely chaotic: The number of bugs swings in a totally erratic way from year to year. Periodic behavior, albeit an infinite number of oscillations, one within the other, has given way to total chaos.

What Is Chaos?

But what is chaos? We have already seen that chaos can be pictured as motion so complex that the ever-changing position and velocity of a particle can only be described using the infinite detail of a fractal strange attractor. The bug equation indicates that chaos is beyond an infinity of cycles, one nested inside the other. But this implies that chaos can no longer be thought of as an absence or lack of order. Rather, it is a new order so rich and subtle that it lies beyond any pattern or periodicity. Chaos is an order of infinite complexity; indeed, if one wanted to pin down a chaotic system, an infinite amount of information and detail would be required.

The bug equation, also called the Verhulst equation, is the simplest possible nonlinear equation, yet it has a truly staggering range of behaviors. It has been applied to everything from insect populations in orchards to the speed with which people learn to the spread of rumors to the movement of genes through different populations. Just as the complexity in a tiny region of a turbulent river arises from its sensitivity to all the water flowing around it, so, too, the complexity of the insect population arises from its constant iteration, as the eggs of a previous year's population are fed back as input for this year.

The effect could be compared with the way a baker works with dough, for it contains two factors—one that causes the population to expand and the other that makes it decrease. Likewise, the baker stretches out the dough and then folds it over. Imagine a face drawn in the dough. Nearby features on the face are stretched out and folded back on themselves so that after many iterations the original face becomes profoundly distorted. So, too, with an insect population in which the competing factors of increase and decrease are fed back to produce everything from oscillation to chaos.

The Verhulst equation and the strange attractor are both deterministic, the result of unitary, iterative processes. Indeed, chaos theory is essentially a deterministic theory of nature and raises the question, Can a deterministic theory truly capture the essence of nature's chaos? A similar issue has already been raised in the case of fractals, for despite their infinite detail, it is not clear if they are a faithful representation of the subtlety and authenticity of natural forms. Likewise, one could ask, Is there, perhaps, an element of the irrational in nature, something fine enough to swim through the net of deterministic chaos theory? The idea that nature is inherently nonunitary would also imply that chaos theory is only an approximation to something far deeper. Nevertheless, at the moment it is the best that science has to offer, and it certainly provides a rich series of images and metaphors for complexity.

▣ Infinite Sensitivity

What is particularly notable about the Verhulst equation is its extreme sensitivity in the chaotic region. This has profound implications for the way humans seek to impose control over the natural world. Suppose, for example, that you gather data to produce a table of future insect populations. You feed this year's population into the equation, say, 0.34585637, and start calculating. But what about the final digit in that initial value—the 7? How do you know if the actual population is really 0.345856372 and not 0.345856376? Because our pocket calculator allows for the input of only eight digits, there is always some uncertainty in that last figure: Is it closer to 7 or 8? Yet who in everyday life worries about the last figure on a calculator? If you are a millionaire, such an error would only amount to one cent when adding up all your assets.

But remember that this value is used as the input to calculate next year's population, and the result of that calculation is then fed back as input for the following year. So even a tiny initial error or uncertainty will circle back in the equation, being stretched and folded, year after year. As time goes on, the reiteration of a tiny error magnifies and accumulates to the point where it eventually swamps the actual population of insects. In fact, it turns out that a pocket calculator is really too crude when it comes to making predictions from the Verhulst equation, for even after a few decades, the calculated predictions of insect populations would be totally useless, swamped by that tiny error in the last figure.

But what about a computer that works to sixteen figures? It turns out that after only fifty years the uncertainty in the last figure, which amounts to an error of only one part in ten quadrillion (a one followed by sixteen zeroes), will have grown to dominate the calculation. We will have no idea of the population of insects in the fifty-first year simply because of an almost infinitesimal uncertainty in counting the original population!

And this tells us something of great importance about chaos:

Although its internal processes may be deterministic, this really does not help us in predicting the future, for even the very smallest uncertainty in measuring a system's properties will rapidly become stretched out to the point where all predictions are useless. It is like those two cars that entered a highway at rush hour together and half an hour later found themselves to be many miles apart. The slightest difference in the point of entry makes a profound difference as to where the cars end up.

The nonlinear behavior of the population equation implies that such systems are extraordinarily sensitive to any external influence. Suppose that in counting the number of bugs in your garden you step on one of them—within a decade or so, the implications of this single act will dominate the entire insect population. Edward Lorenz, one of the first experts to study nonlinear effects in the weather, called this the "butterfly effect"—weather systems are so sensitive that the flapping of a butterfly's wings can change tomorrow's weather.

So even the act of observing or studying an infinitely sensitive system can change its behavior, which means that externalities can never be totally neglected. Also, it is not possible to draw rigid boundaries around such systems and neglect what lies outside, for the smallest external fluctuation may ultimately have an overwhelming effect on the behavior of our system. In general, such systems, through their sensitivity to every part of the landscape, are truly holistic and cannot be fragmented or reduced to simpler independent entities.

▩ Intermittency

There is even more to learn from this simplest of nonlinear equations, for within regions of pure chaos, tiny islands of order can sometimes be seen. These regions indicate a form of behavior that is called *intermittency* and mean that deep within the midst of chaos simple order can still be found. Simple oscillations appear within chaotic fluctuations; they suggest that such order is actually being born out of chaos, rather than chaos out of order.

oscillations appear within chaotic fluctuations; they suggest that such order is actually being born out of chaos, rather than chaos out of order.

Intermittency has been discovered in a wide variety of systems. It is present as occasional periods of silence within the "white noise" of an electronic amplifier or in regions of calm within disturbed water. Short periods of perfect order can manifest themselves in the heart of chaos. For a few moments, chaos ceases and order unfolds, but then chaos reappears again. What is even more surprising is that the intervals, in time, between chaos and order may themselves have a fractal structure!

Intermittency is characteristic of so many natural systems that one also begins to wonder about social systems. Are periods of social calm really the norm, or are they an unfolding out of a more basic chaos? We are used to thinking of chaos as being the disruption of good order by some external disturbance. But what if the reverse were true? What if chaos, that is, a highly complex order, prevails and what we take for simple order is really the unfolding of one aspect of this underlying complexity?

The insights of chaos theory challenge us to transcend the traditional duality between chaos and order. After all, when a society enters a period of what is called "chaos," it becomes increasingly sensitive to its environment and to its own inner order. Out of such infinite complexity, in which each sector of society becomes critically aware of all other aspects of the whole, can be born new social forms and orders.

A society could move, in a creative way, between times of regular order and periods in which that simple order gives way to highly complex transitions in which each member of society feels increasingly aware of his or her own role and position and of current values and social orders. To those in power, who wish at all costs to retain the earlier order, this will appear to be a period of social disruption; yet provided that too much energy or violence is not used to suppress this transition period, out of it can grow a new order. So periods of social transition need not necessarily be negative things, nor need they be the result of external conflicts and challenges, for they may arise out of the natural internal dynamics of that society. Within certain social contexts, intermittency could therefore be the healthy norm.

▋ Bifurcations

Another example of the complex landscape of a nonlinear system is called a *bifurcation point*. Close to a normal attractor, we can perturb a system and have it always return to its limit cycle or limit point. But push it too far up a mountain, and it may reach a ridge or peak, a critical region in which the system faces a decision: It can either fall back to its limit cycle or roll down the other side of the mountain into some qualitatively new region of behavior (Figure 7.14).

Nature abounds in examples of such bifurcation or decision points—regions in which the tiniest push can force a system to go one way or the other. Its systems can move very quickly from stability to instability, from order to chaos, from oscillation to wild fluctuation, from self-correction to infinite sensitivity.

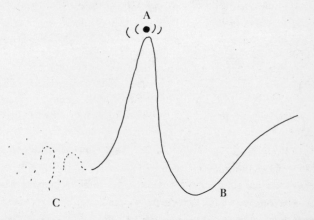

Figure 7.14. The system has reached a bifurcation point *A*. The slightest perturbation may cause it to fall to the right, where it becomes trapped in an attractor basin, *B*. An infinitesimal perturbation to the left will cause it to fall toward the strange attractor *C* when it is gripped by chaotic motion.

Implications

More and more, scientists are discovering that nonlinearity is the norm, whereas truly linear systems are the exception in nature or are crude approximations to more subtle nonlinear behavior. Nonlinear systems include those in which what happens in one region depends sensitively on another region and, in turn, feeds back to it; in which what happens this year is fed back to produce next year's result; in which different parts behave cooperatively; and in which the whole engages in a sort of dance. In short, they are systems that exhibit holistic behavior. Since their landscape can be so rich and varied, it is worth summarizing the properties of their various regions:

1. Bifurcation points lie between regions of qualitatively different behavior. At such points, the system becomes excessively sensitive to the smallest perturbation.
2. Regions within the influence of a normal attractor show (a) excessive stability and resistance to change (a limit point) and (b) the possibility of stable oscillations (a limit cycle).
3. Regions influenced by a strange attractor show (a) random, chaotic, and infinitely complex motion; (b) infinite sensitivity to the environment; (c) behavior so complex as to be unpredictable; and (d) infinite levels of detail within the motion and the possibility of self-similarity at all scales.
4. Systems that iterate or feed back into themselves can exhibit a wide range of behavior from stability to chaos. In addition, the complicated dynamics of such systems may be generated internally rather than as the result of external forces.

Other aspects of behavior that have not been touched on in this chapter include such things as:

- Solitons
- Feedback and feedforward systems
- Ilya Prigogine's dissipative structures
- René Thom's catastrophe theory[5]

We have seen how systems can spontaneously generate their own orders and forms and, in the previous chapter, how they can enter into subtle forms of communication with each other and with their surrounding environment. It is as if each natural system were floating in an ocean of active information or were part of a living hologram.

So nature is a vast and complex dynamic landscape that demands maps that are much closer to those discussed at the start of this book than to the rigid and mechanical blueprints of a linear machine. Something of the complexity of this landscape has been revealed in the present chapter using the insights of chaos theory. Admittedly, chaos theory is unitary and deterministic and, therefore, only a pale shadow of the much deeper nonunitary orders that are possible within nature. Nevertheless, it has revealed something about the wide range of behavior, from stable oscillation to infinitely sensitive chaos, that can be expected from a natural system. The implications of nature's sensitivity and complexity will be explored in the final chapter of this book, where a new sort of action and a new way of being within the universe will be revealed.

CHAPTER EIGHT

GENTLE ACTION FOR A HARMONIOUS WORLD

This book paints new maps of the world, picturing a universe in which each atom, rock, and star drinks of the same boundless waters of creativity. Nature is a symphony in which new themes, harmonies, and structures are ever-unfolding. These structures and processes remain in constant communication with each other and engage in a dance of form. Life swims in an ocean of meaning, in an activity and coherence that blur the distinctions between the animate and the inanimate, between thought and matter.

New values and meanings unfold from this map, for as participators in a living universe, we are called to a new way of acting and being. We can no longer treat nature in a mechanical way, as we have done in the past. Indeed, a whole new social order is called for. The question of what this new order could be, together with other implications of this new map of nature, is explored in this final chapter.

The Tree of Life

While a machine preserves its structure through the very strength and rigidity of its parts, a living system must constantly adjust if it is to survive. Life can be compared with a fountain playing in a city square, for its security lies within the fact of its constant change—the continuous flow of water. If a fountain were to hold on to a particular moment, the result would be its immediate destruction. Likewise, the vortex in the river remains stable by being continually open to the flowing river. Life is constant movement, a flame of being constantly fed and renewed.

The tree that has stood for five hundred years is a vortex within a constantly flowing movement. Despite its apparent solidity, the tree is open to its environment: Through its leaves, it exchanges gases such as oxygen, carbon dioxide, and water vapor. The sun's energy falls on each leaf and powers the complex chemical reactions that provide the tree with its nourishment. Water and minerals enter its roots and flow up the trunk to the leaves. Sugars made in the leaves return to the body of the tree.

Just as a vortex is sustained by the water that flows through it, so a tree is sustained by the water that flows from the earth, the air that enters its leaves, and the sun that beats down on it. Seen from one perspective, the tree represents stability, but at another level, the tree is in constant response, and there is no absolute boundary where the tree ends and earth, air, and sunlight begin.

The life and stability of tree, fountain, candle flame, river vortex, society, and human being lie in openness to the external world and the ability to make delicate and ever-changing movements and adjustments. To borrow a phrase, life "goes with the flow."

Much of what our present society does is very different from this. To a great extent, we have separated ourselves from nature and believe that we are the crown of creation, with the whole world arranged for our exploitation and use. Indeed, we have cast ourselves in the role of heroes who struggle against the natural order and seek to overcome all adversities so that we can grasp the world's riches.

▓ From Tragedy to Comedy

Ecologist and writer Joseph W. Meeker has pointed out that the concept of tragedy and the heroic struggle is particular to our Western civilization, running from Sophocles through Shakespeare to the present day. The literature and stories of other cultures, however, tend to focus around the opposite pole, comedy. A hero pits himself (generally, the hero is masculine) against the gods in a struggle that may end in death and the suffering of his subjects. By contrast, comedy is concerned with the day-to-day survival of ordinary people, not through confrontation but by playing within the scope of nature's rules and dancing around them. While the hero is noble and clings to fixed rules of behavior, comedy is lively, bawdy, concerned with the reversal of roles, fertility, and the ultimate absurdity of human authority. Whereas tragedy culminates in death, comedy ties its knots in a marriage and never ends.

Meeker points out that our planet can no longer afford to support a heroic society, one that seeks to dominate the natural world and struggle against its laws. He calls instead for a "comedy of survival," a spirit of creative play that vitalizes our daily lives and moves outward into society. Our society must learn to swim in the currents of the world. Like the tree, it must remain open to change and ever able to adjust. We must realize that what is fixed is always provisional and defined only within certain limits and contexts. Our internal and collective maps must remain in harmony with the reality of the external world and embrace a totally new ethic and way of being.

▓ Control or Illusion?

When I was a student, I drove a very old car called a Ford Prefect. It had a simple design and a habit of breaking down in out-of-the-way places. But in those days, you could purchase a booklet that offered a variety of diagnostic tests. If the car shuddered to a halt, all you had to do was open the book and follow the directions. The first step was to figure out if the problem arose in the electrical system or in the fuel system. Determining which one was faulty ruled out the other system. For example, if the electricals were working, then probably the right fuel mixture was not reaching the cylinders. Did the problem lie between the carburetor and the fuel pump? The booklet offered a series of tests for each step in the fuel supply.

In order to write the booklet, the author had pictured an automobile as a set of logical connections—an interlocking causal chain. By following a logical path through this system, it was possible to discover, for example, if the breakdown was the result of a blocked fuel needle valve in the carburetor. Once the defect had been located, it was simply a matter of repairing or replacing that part and starting the car again.

In the world of my Ford Prefect, every problem could be localized to a particular cause, and every difficulty had a prescribed cause of action. Even the act of adjusting any one part had a predictable outcome on the car's overall performance. There were no surprises in this world, no problems that could not be cured, no form of behavior that could not be accounted for. The diagnostic booklet provided an accurate map of a real automobile and its behavior.

▋ A Web of Connection

The real world is nothing like an automobile, yet in many ways, we continue to behave as if it were. Faced with an economic fluctuation, we focus on one part of a complex and interlocking world—the economy—and begin our analysis. We jump to the conclusion that any deviation must be called "a problem" and that every problem has a localizable cause in some defect or error that can eventually be put right. The solution to every problem is an action that will bring the world back on track.

But this approach only works in very limited contexts. Earlier chapters showed that natural systems, including societies, have a vast landscape of behavior that ranges from stability and oscillation to chaos and infinite sensitivity. While it may be possible to manage a system within that certain narrow range in which its behavior can be more easily mapped and the result of an intervention may be predicted, push that system too far and it may reach a bifurcation point where it will jump to some radically different form of behavior. Other systems may lie beyond any attempt at simple description, and the effects of intervention will be totally unpredictable. Some systems are so sensitive that it is impossible to separate them from the wider context in which they are embedded. Others may be too stable and rigid to change. Some systems change in direct response to external conditions, others as an expression of their own internal dynamics.

The essential paradox is that the natural world is far more complex, subtle, and rapid in its responses than the organizations that attempt to control it. Organizations contain internal rigidities and fixed responses, their maps are fragmented, their range of behavior is limited and slow. An organization that attempts to control the natural world is like a somnambulist on a runaway horse.

Organizations focus on limited domains and are geared to act in similarly limited ways. How can they deal with issues that spread out in complicated ways over whole areas of society and the globe? The destruction of the Brazilian rain forest, for example, is the result of a vast web of issues including international debt, economics, and global values. North America's love of beef has an influence on the profitability of raising cattle, so the sale of hamburgers in Detroit may influence a Brazilian rancher to seek more land. This, of course, is a fairly direct connection. But think of the astronomical number of social, economic, political, environmental, ethical, and even religious issues that trace their way toward a particular situation within the Brazilian rain forest. Ask which issues can safely be ignored and which are important. Ask how far away a country must be and how small its gross national product before it has a negligible effect on the way of life of a tribe living within that rain forest?

As another example, take the apparently straightforward decision to buy a new automobile. You own an old gas guzzler, and friends, concerned about energy consumption, urge you to trade in your car for a smaller model with a highly efficient engine. This act, they say, will save hundreds of gallons of gasoline each year.

At first sight, trading in your old car seems a sensible decision. But wait a moment. That new car takes energy to prepare and mold the metals and plastics that are used in its construction and to power the factory where it is assembled. Would it be better to burn gasoline in your present inefficient automobile or incur the capital energy costs needed to build a new model?

And does it even make sense to compare different energy sources like gasoline with the various forms of energy required to create an automobile? Some of that latter energy may come from a hydroelectric plant, from a nuclear reactor, or from coal. How are renewable and nonrenewable energy sources to be compared? And what about the whole question of economic, social, and political structures surrounding the production and distribution of gasoline as well as other forms of energy? But is energy consumption the only question? What of the social, economic, environmental, and political implications of automobile manufacture? Where is the automobile made? What sector of the world's population is touched by its manufacture? Where do its components come from? What impact does each automobile make on the environment?

These are some of the questions one could ask about the decision to buy a new car. And each question is directly connected to a host of others that expand ever outward, touching a host of seemingly unrelated issues. In fact, I doubt if anyone knows the correct answer to that dilemma about buying a new automobile. Indeed, the whole notion of "the correct answer" may in itself be a mistake.

A sophisticated computer analysis of all energy pathways

provides a partial answer but only at the expense of ignoring a host of other environmental and social issues. And who knows if any one of those other connections may not, in some complex way, feed back into the whole domain of energy production and use? Within some limited contexts, it may be possible to arrive at a rational decision and determine a course of action. But who knows if at the time that decision was made an action taken somewhere else in the world may spread out in a subtle way and modify the whole context under which the original decision was made?

Every day we make decisions within a vast and ever-changing matrix of interconnections. Even the choice of whether to drink tea or coffee has global implications. In certain countries, coffee is a major export, so that the smallest fluctuation in international coffee futures may have a devastating impact on its economy. Indeed, when coffee prices fall, the result may be the difference between subsistence and starvation and, for some farmers, the first step toward being drawn into the international drug market.

Action or Paralysis?

The world today faces a number of major crises, problems that appear so serious and situations whose balance is so critical that they cry out for action. Yet, as we have now seen, action that is not intelligently guided can lead to even worse problems, for the whole nature of the organizations is too crude to meet the infinite subtlety of the very systems they are designed to control.

This is the essential paradox of action: When we act, we do so blindly and in limited ways, out of ignorance and partial understanding, and from a fragmented basis with no true indication of the implications of what we do. Yet if we do not act, we become impotent and things get totally out of control—the dilemma that has faced individuals and governments throughout the ages. At best, we try to do what looks right at the time and hope that if we do make a mess, someone else will clean it up. But the world is getting smaller, and the implications of our mistakes are ever more deadly. Everyone, from the individual in a family to the head of state who ponders the problems of the world, is caught in this paradox of action.

Creative Suspension

There is a way of transcending this paradox. It lies in not being trapped in that oscillation between action and paralysis by moving beyond them to their common source. I will call this way beyond by the names of *creative suspension* and *active watchfulness*. This suggests that through seeking the timeless moment that lies between intent and action, one can come into contact with a whole structure of thought, the disposition of mind and body, and limited patterns of rigidities and response.

What is creative suspension? Simply put, in the face of an urgent demand for action, or the desire for an immediate response, one seeks an infinitesimal region of watchful silence.

Think of some of the most urgent things that could ever face us, like being involved in a traffic accident, a violent crime, or a house fire. In such cases, paralysis or an instinctive reaction is often the rule; both can prove equally disastrous.

Imagine an overturned automobile with a shattered windshield. A driver sits silently behind the wheel, and in the passenger seat, someone with a bloody face is screaming. Where you or I may rush forward and try to help the injured person, the immediate action of a good doctor is not to touch or intervene but simply to use his or her eyes. The doctor observes and attempts to make sense of the scene. Things may not be as obvious as they appeared at first sight. The passenger may be in great pain or simply in a hysterical state with superficial wounds. The silent driver, however, may be frozen in a state of shock caused by serious internal injuries.

A good physician begins in a state of watchful suspension,

using eyes and ears. Only then does the doctor reach out and very gently touch the injured person. Little by little, the doctor makes a series of exploratory actions, small movements of the hands and eyes. Only when the doctor has a fairly good idea of the extent of the injuries involved and the state of the accident victim is physical intervention advisable. To attempt to move a person, administer an injection, or manipulate part of the body may complicate an already delicate situation.

The suspension, on the part of a good doctor, of immediate reaction leads to a state of heightened awareness and a deeper understanding of the overall situation. But there is more to creative suspension than this, for it can be a way of getting in touch with one's whole pattern of reactions, rigidities, limited structures and conditioning, and for that matter, the rigidities within an organization.

In this sense, active watchfulness has echoes of the various systems of meditation practiced in the East. Through meditation, one seeks to reach the source of thoughts and watch them arise and die. In creative suspension, the idea is to observe the whole nature of intention, action, and conditioning by momentarily not giving animation to the intention to act or to carry out a thought. Through an alert form of watchfulness, it becomes possible to perceive how this intention unfolds and acts through the mind and body.

As an example, suppose someone calls you an insulting name. Your natural reaction may be either to hit back or to control yourself in an effort to rise above the situation. If you choose the latter, you appear outwardly calm yet notice a quickening of the pulse and a faltering in your breathing. There will also be a flurry of thoughts, which you attempt to calm down or suppress. Indeed, in trying to appear normal and untroubled, you may be driven to say something inappropriate and make the situation even worse.

Hit back or swallow the insult? One is trapped, in fact, in the same paradox as the world leader who is faced with a crisis and wonders whether to act or play for time. But there is a way of transcending this dilemma by allowing an infinitesimal gap in which the whole intention to act, or suppress, is allowed to expand and work its way through the mind and body. Rather than seeking outward expression, or suppression, of this intention, one feels, listens to, watches, and attends to its act of unfolding. Creative suspension allows you to observe the way that certain words evoke a physical reaction within your body and how this physical reaction can, in turn, trigger other thoughts and words or modify their meanings.

To allow a gap between intention and action is to expose the whole structure of thought and conditioning within mind and body. The gap may be so short that it lies beyond time, a timeless instant of suspension that enables the mind to touch a creative perception, to enter into a new order.

Movement Without Motion

The complex nature of intention, which is watched during creative suspension, can be illustrated by the following example. Israeli physicist-turned-therapist Moshe Feldenkrais taught a form of physical and mental activity aimed at breaking down the conditioned blocks of responses within the body and substituting new, more subtle movements. Many therapists have taught that physical and mental traumas are stored not only as memories but also as muscular tensions and fixed patterns of physical response within the body. A fixed thought manifests itself as a muscular disposition, and a pattern of body tensions can enfold a memory.

But it is of little help to tell people to change the way they sit or walk. Feldenkrais's method was to break down the old complexes of movement and allow the body and mind to learn new and more subtle dispositions through, as I interpret it, exploring the operation of intention.

In a Feldenkrais session, the therapist asks the patient not so much to move in a certain fashion as to generate the intention to move. For example, the patient may be asked to carry out a fairly complex and unfamiliar pattern of movements. Different parts of the body carry out very different sorts of movements that are not understandable through the usual way in which simple movements are strung together to create complex series of steps. In fact, the patient may not be able to imagine the motion in any rational, logical way. Nevertheless, in some more intuitive fashion, the mind generates the intention to duplicate this whole pattern of movement.

It is quite surprising how, at this level, the mind and body work together to evolve such a highly complicated and flexible pattern of movement to replace the body's simpler and more rigid conditioning. It suggests that our capacity for creating new and highly subtle responses may be far greater than we realize. For once we free ourselves of fixed patterns and blocks, we will tap into an unlimited source of creativity.

It turns out that actualizing this new and complex intention as physical movements of the body is not that important. Indeed, according to Feldenkrais's practice, the smaller and more minimally these movements are made, the better. It is as if the physical movement already exists as a sort of potential or as a subtly enfolded order within the brain and body. Actual patterns of movement seem to be encoded in the form of minimal signals involving muscles and nervous systems, electrical and chemical memories, dispositions, sensitivities, and potentiality. Intention is a highly complex web, a sort of information that can, at any moment, move from being potential to active.

Making a movement allows this active potentiality to unfold in a perfectly natural way through physical action. Yet in another sense, before it is done, the motion already exists and has been experienced within the body in its potential form.

Unfolding the Intention

Creative suspension could be thought of as the obverse to this building up of potential action into intention. Rather than being directed toward outward action, creative suspension seeks the inward unfolding of the whole complex pattern that is implicit within the intention to take action. It is as if one were able to display within the silent, watching mind and body the whole pattern of thought and disposition that is directed into an external activity and, along with it, the nature and structure of one's rigidities and conditioning at the personal, emotional, and social levels.

Just as it is possible for a person to create inwardly the whole intention to a new external action, so, too, it may be possible to display inwardly and explicitly the detailed structure inherent in a given pattern of response. This inward display therefore gives us an insight into the limits of our response within a given situation. Through a creative act of perception, we can free ourselves from limiting aspects of our conditioning and move to a more fluid response.

Listening to the Organization

Creative suspension allows us to listen to our personal responses and to occupy a new space in which something faster and more creative can operate. What applies to the individual is relevant to an organization and society as a whole.

Faced with a serious crisis, an organization feels the immediate need to react. In a limited and more concrete sense, it is clear that the effect of a momentary suspension of outwardly directed action would be to plunge an organization into a flurry of internal activity. Urgent messages would be exchanged by the various officials, and a variety of directives would flash across the screens of computer terminals in the various offices.

But the idea of creative suspension is not to "do nothing" or to block external activity but rather to enter into an alert state of watchfulness in which individuals and groups within the organization become aware of the tensions, motivations, plans, goals, responses, and values that cause them to take action. A person may observe, for example, how the directives inherent in a particular mandate unfold as they flow through the organization or become blocked and transformed. In this fashion, the whole dynamics of an organization, with its patterns of communication, centers of activity, and channels of response, becomes transparent. The whole nature of the organization is exposed along with its areas of rigidity and conditioned behavior.

Increased awareness touches not only surface structures and lines of communication but also the significant values, motives, and beliefs that are buried within an organization. And just as a plasma or a slime mold is both a collective whole and a number of individuals, so an organization is enfolded in groups, corporate structures, lines of communication, and human individuals. Creative suspension operates at all these levels, right down to each person within an organization, with his or her particular needs, values, and desire for security, satisfaction, and creative challenge.

Through creative suspension, an organization, and each person in it, becomes increasingly sensitive to the whole nature of its thoughts and actions and in so doing dissolves fixed forms and patterns—or rather, it no longer supports them and gives them energy. The result is a transformation of what a group or organization means and does.

Each of us touches a ground of limitless creativity whose outflowing is blocked by our fixed patterns of response and complexes of thought. But now we see a way of dissolving these blocks and allowing creativity to flower. Indeed, the possibility is raised that the internal dynamics of an organization or individual can become as infinitely sensitive and creative as the world outside.

The way an organization views the world also changes, for our perceptions are colored by internal preconceptions. We see what we expect to see and give attention to what has most value to us. And in breaking free from past conditionings and moving within ever-changing contexts, our sensitivity to the outside world increases. The more aware we are to what happens within, the more we perceive the world outside.

The paradox of action is that in so many ways nature lies

beyond total analysis so that no fixed plan can ever match the subtlety and richness of the external world. But now it becomes possible to transcend boundaries and internalize the endless complexity of the world. Rather than seeking to control and predict events, it becomes possible to play out new possibilities within an organization or individual. The ever-changing dynamics of the world are mirrored, or inwardly projected, into the organization, and out of this, a totally new form of action is born.

Gentle Action

When seeking to control something, one sits outside the object, views it as a separate entity, and tries to manipulate it according to a preconceived goal or plan. But once the barriers between inner and outer, inscape and landscape, are dissolved, and fixed responses give way to fluid and complex actions, then a new form of active perception can be practiced. The outflowing from this holistic perception is what I will call *gentle action*.

Let me first give an image of what this gentle action could be. Conventional action tends to be applied locally and directly to the source of the problem. The more serious the problem, the stronger must be this corrective force. Gentle action, by contrast, involves extremely subtle actions that are widely distributed over the whole system. Rather than attacking a problem head on, gentle action seeks its source, which may have no single location or simple structure.

Gentle action could be compared with the act of floating in an ocean, where one continually makes tiny movements and adjustments. Almost unconsciously one's active awareness keeps the body floating on its back. Even resting in bed, one is sending out small exploratory signals to the muscles, which barely tense and flex in reaction. However, the feedback from these muscular explorations moves through the body and gives us a sense of our exact orientation in the bed.

When floating in the ocean, these tiny movements extend

into the water until we become one with the ocean and its every movement. Gentle action not only gives us a picture of the ocean and our relationship to it, but it is the very action that keeps us afloat. Gentle action is an extension of creative suspension, for it is a way of both feeling out the world and adjusting to its flow.

▓ Splashes and Ripples

Normal action is like a heavy stone thrown into a pond. It produces a big splash in one particular region and a large number of ripples as a by-product. What, for example, would such action mean in the context of a group concerned about the destruction of a region of a hypothetical rain forest?

A group presses for immediate action, and as public support mounts, the government passes legislation to prevent the cutting down of more trees. But this does not prove effective, for there are a variety of vested interests at stake. However, as public reaction becomes more vocal, police move in and make arrests among people who are doing the logging. At this point, the situation escalates. A local official is shot, someone else disappears and in a matter of days, troops are called in. The end result is that logging is stopped and the forest is saved—but only for the time being. A decade later, extreme poverty in that region precipitates a bloody revolution that no one could have foreseen. Little can now be done to save the forest. Was there an alternative to throwing that first rock into the water?

To pursue the metaphor, let me propose something very curious that lies outside our everyday experience of the world. Suppose that all around the edge of the pond you create tiny ripples. Their movement is barely noticeable, and they quickly die out and become lost in the general chance disturbances of the pond. But create these ripples again, this time in such a way that the phase of each one is exactly coordinated with all the others. Now the ripples can engage in a dance that extends throughout the pond, for like the dance of electrons in a superconductor, the ripples are part of a greater whole.

To see how this can happen, think back to the double-slit experiment in which the interference of waves behind the slits leads to a pattern of light and dark regions. The same thing happens when ripples meet in a pond: Where crests encounter crests, the result is an increased disturbance, and where crests and troughs meet, the effect cancels out. In our everyday world, a collection of tiny ripples is never sufficiently coherent, or co-ordinated in a precise way, so that the overall effect of interference is to produce random patterns in the water that soon die out.

But with a totally precise coordination in time and space, each tiny ripple can interfere in a constructive way and enhance the effect of its neighbor. The resulting ripples grow in size as they move inward. Imperceptible disturbances at the edge of the pond become a circular wave that converges, growing in intensity as it moves, so that by the time it reaches the center of the pond, it produces a large, focused splash.

The results look like the time reversal of the more conventional outward-spreading splash. Indeed, they appear to defy common sense, for we simply do not see such things in our everyday world. The reason is that to bring about this effect requires an incredibly subtle and complex coordination around the edge of the pond, an unimaginably precise activity of global information. It is exactly this same coordinated global activity that is involved in gentle action.

Let us move from metaphor to actuality, from a pond to a rain forest. The idea of gentle action as applied to a rain forest would be a very delicate activity that is not specifically focused on the rain forest as such but arises out of a sensitive perception of its much wider matrix of connections, interactions, and implications. The decisions made by a Japanese banker, an American teenager at a hamburger stand, a British car salesperson, a newspaper columnist in Berlin, a coffee broker, and a person switching channels between TV shows may, in extremely subtle ways, affect the life of a peasant farmer who lives on the edge of a rain forest. Just as a splash can begin around the edge of a pond, so, in its most fundamental sense, the action that will save a rain forest, decrease infant mortality, or reduce urban crime must begin in a precisely coordinated multiplicity of different ways and locations.

Gentle action is global. It arises out of the whole nature and structure of a particular issue. It addresses itself not just to practical issues, such as the price of oil or the efficiency of a given factory, but also to values, ethics, and the quality of life. Gentle action begins in a highly intelligent and coordinated fashion within a wide variety of situations. And like the ripples around the point, it moves inward to converge on a particular issue. Gentle action works not through force and raw energy but by modifying the very processes that generate and sustain an undesired or harmful effect.

The implications of gentle action are far-reaching. The problems that face us today call for the transformation of people's lives and values as well as the very conditions under which they live. By transcending our traditional responses with their desire for security and control, we can act in ways that are sensitive to the whole complex dynamics of the situation itself.

Nonlocal Action

Gentle action can also be thought of as nonlocal because it unfolds in a generative way out of many different locations to converge on a particular region. By contrast, physics has tended to look at the world in terms of causal chains that are directly connected by pushes and pulls and through fields and interactions that move outward from a given point.

As an example of global coordination, think of massed bands and choirs in a great arena. You occupy the best seat in the house, yet when the conductor's baton lifts, something curious happens: The music is not quite right—some of the players sound as if they are coming in after the beat. While all the musicians started on time, the sounds coming from those who are far away take longer to travel than from those nearby. Musicians in a distant band sound as if they are half a beat behind those right in front of you.

The only way in which such music would sound perfectly coordinated to your ears would be to have each musician hit the beat at a slightly different instant. The total order of the music only appears when all the musicians are coordinated in this way. This could, in fact, be done in a relatively mechanical way. But what happens if you start moving around the auditorium so that your distance from each musician keeps changing? And what if the musicians themselves are also moving? In order to preserve perfect order to your ears, each musician would have to be constantly changing the instant at which he or she hit the beat, and this could only be done through an ever-changing pattern of global information. In a sense, the order of the music would unfold from a nonlocal correlation of all the musicians, an effect that could be compared with the operation of gentle action.

We have already met something analogous to this in the overall global form of the wave function that coordinates the motion of each electron in a superconductor. In a normal metal, the wave function is not coherent but composed of the many individual contributions from each tiny region. In a superconductor, however, the entire wave function coheres. The overall, global form of the wave function acts to guide the motion of each individual electron. Likewise, gentle action arises out of the overall form of a given situation.

▪ Gentle Action and the Quantum Potential

The way a major change can be brought about through an infinitesimal but highly intelligent action can be compared with David Bohm's quantum potential. Bohm has pointed out that unlike the mechanical pushes and pulls exerted by the fields and forces of conventional physics the quantum potential acts as a guide. His example of the ocean liner shows how subtle information in a radio or radar signal acts to give form to the raw energy of the engines. The information that is enfolded within the quantum potential is similarly rich and arises out of the whole context of the quantum system. It acts, for example, to guide an electron through one of the double slits.

In a similar way, gentle action does not apply force to achieve a particular effect. Rather, it works within the very level that generates that particular effect. As with the quantum potential, it does not so much push and pull as it gives form to a particular level of unfolding, for gentle action arises out of a creative perception of a complex situation. Gentle action could therefore be compared with the imperceptible movements a high-wire artist uses to maintain balance and harmony—no heroic large measures are used to keep aloft.

Social Action

Gentle action unfolds globally out of the many different levels within a system and gives a new dimension to the whole idea of social action. It suggests that the origins of effective action can lie with ordinary people, both as individuals and as members of a group—and with their values, ethics, goals, and desires. Rather than the origin of social change being always found in a political official policy, it can begin within individuals and unfold through organizations and governments. It can be a change in consumer habits, a new consciousness of ethical issues, or a feeling of increased identity and worth.

Governments sometimes act like the rock thrown into the pond when they take direct and forceful measures to resolve an issue. But it is possible to see government officials in a new light—not as prime movers in themselves but as points of focus. Just as the splash in a pond is produced by a large rock or generated by tiny correlated ripples, so, too, gentle action can unfold and animate a particular action or transformation.

People sometimes feel discouraged in the face of political

power, for they constitute only one voice among millions. Yet through gentle action, we realize how the values and wishes and intentions of each individual can be crucial. The individual can be a tiny but precisely coordinated ripple that contributes to a much greater wave. For without each ripple to play its part in a much greater global action, the whole wave would die. No longer can political power be measured by force, finances, or number of votes; the actions of each individual are important in a variety of unforeseen ways.

These ideas point to a new meaning for society, a society with rich and detailed maps and a highly subtle order that does not support fixed forms or hierarchies but that operates in a sensitive, organic way.[1] Just as the cell and organism can be pictured as a dance of meaning and communication, so, too, can society and the individual. This relationship has been compared with the relationship between the electron and the plasma, in which the behavior of each is enfolded within the other. Likewise, ethics, goals, meanings, and values would be mutually enfolded within society and the individual.

Brain Dance

Gentle action has applications not only to society but also to biology and physics. The idea that the immune system is a flow of active meaning throughout the body has already been discussed. It can also serve as a new way of looking at the brain.

Compare the generation of thought within the brain to a pattern of ripples on the surface of a pond. But not a simple ring of ripples, as in our earlier metaphor—rather, as highly correlated ripples that are constantly converging and diverging as they dance across the surface of the water. A ripple in one region interferes constructively with others to generate a complicated shape that moves inward. Complexes of ripples oscillate in a sort of breathing, now expanding, now focusing, toward some new region.

Translate this image into the electrochemical activity of the brain, constantly moving across its surface and downward into its deeper levels. Some of these ripples have their generative origin in a particular location and spread over the brain. Others begin in a delocalized way: Individual nerve impulses and chemical flows that are distributed all over the brain converge to a focus within a given region, only to expand outward again.

The constant play of activity across the brain can be related to a number of images such as coherent and collective oscillations whose origins lie in the activity of the whole system or to the way in which the form of a wave function determines individual behavior. It also relates to active information in the quantum potential whereby the form of the whole determines the motion of individual parts. Or to nonlocal connections whereby distant quantum objects remain actively correlated.

We have also seen how a complex intention is generated within the brain and unfolds into complex thoughts and muscular actions. The physical brain extends through the entire nervous system and into the body where it interconnects with the immune system. It may even make sense to suggest that the gentle origin of certain thoughts may be found within the muscles and body organs themselves. Just as troublesome thoughts and feelings can give rise to body tensions, so too certain attitudes and thoughts may unfold out of the muscular disposition of the whole body.

Gentle action involves an overall flow of meaning that is both local and nonlocal. In order to picture the brain's activity, we must go beyond concepts imported from what could be termed *local physics*. A localized approach to the brain considers its activities as originating in a localized stimulus that propagates through a network of neural interconnections. But an additional gentle action may also operate in which large-scale regions of the brain become correlated and sensitized so as to evoke a particular coherent activity. This activity need not begin at one specific site but could be generated globally, converging into some regions and diverging from others. This image of the brain seems far closer to our direct experience of thinking.

Global correlations could occur in a number of ways. Collective oscillations in one region of the brain can generate long-range signals that bring different areas into a new order. There may even be coherent states within the brain that are of a quantum mechanical nature. (This is not to say that the brain is totally quantum mechanical in nature, but it is certainly true that the triggering of a signal in a nerve does involve processes in which quanta of energy are exchanged.) The idea would be that quantum correlations extend across appreciable distances, so that the sensitivity of global areas of the brain is influenced by the form of a collective wave function.

So there are a number of ways in which large-scale correlations and gentle action could operate. Another way of visualizing this is in terms of a strange attractor. As we have seen, a chaotic system is not devoid of order, but it moves in such a highly complex way that it can only be described using an infinite amount of information. The strange attractor is an infinitely detailed global form that controls chaotic motion. So rather than thinking of a strange attractor as something that destroys the order in a system, it could be pictured as the global distribution of very subtle information.

Applying this image to the brain, we see that its activity could be controlled by an extremely subtle level of information. Thought would be the response to that information, in the form of particular foldings and unfoldings of electrochemical activity across the brain. But this means that thought is a relatively crude level of brain activity. Thinking may only be a simple part of what the brain can do, for behind thought there may lie something that is infinitely faster and more subtle in its nature. The evidence from various meditational experiences suggests that indeed something deeper lies beyond thought, and that the brain's capabilities are far greater than anyone suspects.

The image of gentle action also suggests why certain functions of the brain, such as memory, cannot be identified with any particular localized structure.[2] Memory seems to be stored nonlocally, for both localized and widely peppered damage to the human brain does destroy specific memories. It has always been a great puzzle as to how memories are recorded, and we now see how the whole dynamics of memory can be nonlocal, with specific thoughts and memories unfolding out of a gentle action within the brain.[3]

Solitons

Gentle action can also serve as a metaphor in physics. The image of the ripples converging toward the center of a lake seems bizarre because we are used to looking at the world in terms of the way individual parts of a system interact. But this does not mean that such phenomena do not occur in nature. There are, for example, curious waves called *solitons* that—because of their internal co-ordination—are able to preserve their form over long distances without ever dissipating. In a normal wave, the process of dispersion causes tiny wavelets to break away from the main wave at slightly different speeds, which eventually leads to its dissipation. In a soliton, however, nonlinear interactions cause these wavelets to couple together so that when one tries to move ahead the others pull it back. Just as the form of a superconducting wave function prevents individual electrons from scattering and causing electrical resistance, so, too, the overall form of the soliton acts to preserve its internal coherence.

Solitons are found in the air as well as in metals, plasmas, planetary atmospheres, and even nuclear structures. Solitons can be considered both as material structures and as movements of energy. Some researchers believe that solitons are responsible for the long-range exchange of biological energy and for the way nerve impulses are transmitted over long distances without degradation. In each case, the soliton emerges out of the correlation of the whole system and cannot be reduced to a simple interaction of independent parts.

Action and Chaos

Gentle action has a direct relationship with what is normally called chaos. The idea has already been proposed, with regard to the brain, that chaos is an order of such a high degree of complexity that it lies beyond any simple description and requires a global map of infinite detail—a strange attractor.

Chaos is infinitely sensitive and infinitely detailed, and in many cases, it is the door through which one structure leaves and another enters. It is not possible to manage or steer a chaotic system in a conventional fashion because it is infinitely sensitive to all its parts. So rather than trying to force a chaotic system in a particular direction, one has to act globally through the structure of its strange attractor. To live in the heart of chaos would involve constantly making vanishingly small but globally coordinated adjustments. One could not remain outside as controller but would have to enter into the system directly and change the quality of its movement at the source of its actual generation.

Entropy and Gentle Action

Gentle action can also shed light on the meaning of entropy. In its simplest form, entropy has to do with the degree of order in a system. Shuffle a pack of cards, and its suits and values become random. The result is a destruction of the original order, and entropy is said to have increased. Leave a piece of iron out in the rain, and it rusts, a process whereby the regular order of atoms in its metal lattice begins to break down.

Physics holds that left to themselves natural systems move to states of higher entropy. But entropy is more than a simple breakdown in order; it is also associated with a loss of correlations, for unless they are constantly restored, correlations within a system will eventually disappear and the system will move toward disorder.

In many ways, however, this view is oversimplistic. We have already seen a variety of examples in which order emerges spontaneously out of chaos. One of the major voices calling for a more generalized view of entropy has been Ilya Prigogine, who has studied many cases in which order emerges dynamically out of chaos. The whole notion of chaos in physics is still not clear. On the one hand, a particular case of chaos may be nothing more than a series of uncoordinated contingencies. On the other, it may conceal a rich and infinitely complex degree of order that lies beyond conventional description. To say that the order in a system breaks down, or that correlations are lost, may be far from straightforward, for new and more subtle forms of order may be created and nonlocal correlations manifest themselves.

Gentle action indicates a way in which a system that on the surface looks chaotic may be correlated at a deeper level so that its distant parts are ordered nonlocally. What appears to be a simple increase in entropy, or disorder, then, could conceal a more subtle form of order. For example, the inexorable march of entropy dictates that ripples in a pond should dissipate, but we have already seen that subtle, nonlocal correlations cause tiny ripples to grow and move inward in a movement that reverses the normal flow of entropy and time. Clearly, the ideas of order and of entropy must be generalized to take into account ideas such as gentle action and nonlocal correlations.

▉ Localization

In the case of the brain, it has already been suggested that localized phenomena could unfold out of more subtle distributed processes, and it could well be that even distant parts of the universe are correlated and nonlocally connected. Gentle action involves a dance of convergence and divergence in which each region of space becomes both local and nonlocal. The orders of space may be rich in new and subtle ways that lie far beyond the original vision of Descartes and Newton.

Moreover, the idea that each point or local region conceals an endlessly complex structure need not only apply to the space in which we move but to a host of other ways in which the idea of "space" is used—for example, to a complex web of logical connections in a computer, to various social relationships, or to a space of social or economic values. In each case, what looks like a small region, or a simple point, may be the nexus of a whole complex, generative process. This possibility suggests that science must totally revise the way it thinks about such systems, for what are taken to be primitive or featureless elements in an economic or social equation may be the unfolding of underlying implicate forms and processes.

Conclusion

This book began with a call for new maps to guide us on our journey through the universe. We now see that this journey has led us away from limited ideas such as mechanism, causality, locality, unitarity, and regular order toward more subtle notions of nonunitarity, inscape, creativity, rich and subtle orders of space and time, chaos as an infinitely complex order, activities of meaning and information, spontaneous structure, communication that becomes communion, and the breaking down of barriers between life and the inanimate, between mind and matter.

Newer and richer maps have been drawn in which the subtle and delicate are important. Indeed, a key conclusion of this book is that science and society must give their attention to new and subtle movements if we are to perceive, think, and act in more harmonious ways.

Over the last two hundred years, science has been remarkably successful in the way it has revealed order in the world. But the time has come for science to move toward a new level of understanding. Its past history could be compared with that of an artist who prepares a sketch for a landscape. Out of a bewildering array of visual data, the artist selects certain shapes and forms. Lines and masses are emphasized and earlier guidelines erased. The result reflects a particular, graphic level of order in the scene. But the artist moves beyond this sketch, using it as a tool or guide to something that is more subtle and involves gradations of tone, rhythms of lines, and harmonies of color. Similarly, science must move beyond its graphic but oversimplified conceptions in order to explore the extremely subtle and inwardly connected aspects of nature.

In the past, science discovered unity within nature by a process of generalization and by moving from the gross to the subtle. In the eighteenth century, physics was concerned with the properties of matter and its motion and transformation. In the nineteenth century, it became preoccupied with what causes these transformations and began to investigate energy. Gradually, the idea evolved that such different phenomena as heat, electricity, and mechanical work could all be related through the more subtle concept of energy. Indeed, light itself was eventually seen as a form of energy, and the notion of an electromagnetic field was introduced.

In moving from matter to energy, physics was directing its attention from the gross to the more subtle. A similar transition is possible today. One can talk, as David Bohm does, about active information giving form to energy or pursue other ideas that have been discussed in this book such as flow of meaning, gentle action, and nonlocal correlations. In each case, science is focusing on something very delicate and highly intelligent.

These ideas can be extended into the domain of our own lives, for the extremely subtle plays a crucial role in all aspects of nature, and it is important to look beyond the surface of things to the very delicate. Synchronicities and moments of illumination become natural unfoldings of the underlying order of nature. Just as patterns of ripples unfold in the brain or on the surface of a lake, so, too, they can move thoughts, dreams, and external physical events.

By dissolving our rigid patterns of thought and response, we allow something faster and more subtle to operate. Indeed, thought itself may be only a small, and relatively crude, portion of what the mind is capable of. The more we give room to the subtle, the more we come to touch the heart of the universe and drink of its creative waters.

We are called to take up these new maps and begin a journey. As with every journey, the most important thing we will ever do is take that first step.

ENDNOTES

Introduction

1. F. David Peat, *Synchronicity: The Bridge Between Matter and Mind* (New York: Bantam Books, 1987).

2. C. G. Jung, *Synchronicity*, trans. R.F.C. Hull (Princeton, N.J.: Princeton University Press, 1973).

3. A. P. Elkin, *The Australian Aborigines* (New York: Doubleday, 1964).

Chapter 1

1. Abraham Maslow, *The Farther Reaches of Human Nature* (New York: Penguin Books, 1973).

2. Chief Seattle's words have been quoted in many books including *The Portable North American Indian Reader*, edited by Frederick W. Turner (New York: Penguin Books, 1977). It also contains records of speeches made by other Native Americans.

3. Pam Colorado quoting her great-grandfather in "Bridging Native and Western Science," *Convergence* XXI (No. 2/3) 49–72, 1988.

4. There are many other books that explore the Indigenous world views of this continent. While some of these are authentic and respectful, the approach of others may range from patronization to exploitation. Beware of books using the word *primitive* in their subtitles, or in which a contemporary author has himself

or herself portrayed proudly wearing feathers and clutching arm-
fuls of sacred pipes and crystals. Reader should be aware that
some elders are not happy that accounts of certain ceremonies
and visions are being made so readily available. The reader should
also remember that articles such as masks, ceremonial pipes, ka-
china dolls, and so forth, that are sometimes offered for sale are
sacred items and not souvenirs or simply works of art.

The words of Black Elk, the great spiritual teacher of the Oglala
Sioux, can be found in *The Sacred Pipe*, edited by Joseph Epes
Brown (New York: Penguin Books, 1981) and in *Black Elk Speaks*,
edited by John G. Neihardt (New York: Washington Square
Press, 1972). T. C. McLuhan's *Touch the Earth: A Self-Portrait of
Indian Existence* (New York: Pocket Books, 1972) presents Indigenous people through their own words. Dennis Tedlock and Bar-
bara Tedlock's *Teachings from the American Earth: Indian Religion
and Philosophy* (New York: Liveright, 1975); John Grim's *The Shaman: Patterns of Religious Healing Among the Ojibway Indians* (Nor-
man, Oklahoma: University of Oklahoma Press, 1983); and *Native
North American Spirituality of the Eastern Woodlands*, edited by Elis-
abeth Tooker (Mahwah, N.J.: Paulist Press, 1979), can also be
consulted. Bruce Chatwin's *The Songlines*, (New York: Penguin
Books, 1988) is a creative attempt to bridge the maps and landscape of the cultures of the Australian Aboriginal and a Western
writer. Colin M. Turnbull's *The Forest People* (New York: Simon
and Schuster, 1961) is a sensitive attempt to convey the feel of
yet another Indigenous culture, that of the BaMbuti Pygmies.

5. Hugh Brody, *Maps and Dreams: Indians and the British Columbia Frontier* (Vancouver, B.C.: Douglas and McIntyre, 1988).

6. Dürer's vision implies a division between the artist and
nature. It can also be looked upon as a fragmentation of the
masculine and feminine. Notice that in the left hand, feminine,
side of the etching nature can be seen through a window. The
only evidence of the natural world that can be found in the more
restrained, masculine half, is of a plant that is constrained within
its pot by means of sticks. Not only is woman to be stretched on
the grid of perspective but nature itself must be made to conform
to this overall conception of order.

It is interesting that similar explorations of these dualities, of
perspective and actuality, artifice and nature, masculine and feminine, sexuality and sterility, the formal garden and human vio-

lence are to be found in Peter Greenaway's remarkable film *The Draftman's Contract*.

Dürer's meditation on the nature of artistic control and sexuality were pursued in our own century by Marcel Duchamp in two outstanding works that can be seen in Philadelphia's Museum of Art: *The Bride Stripped Bare by Her Bachelors, Even* (also known as the Large Glass) and *Given: 1. The Waterfall, 2. The Illuminating Gas*.

7. The connection between Man's view of Woman, and the scientist's vision of nature is explored in Susan Griffin's *Woman and Nature, the Roaring Inside Her* (New York: Harper and Row, 1980).

8. *Die Analyse der Empfindungen und das Verhältnis des Physischen zum Psychischen* first appeared in 1886 under a slightly different title and in four subsequent editions underwent important modifications and expansions.

9. Historically, Newton may not have been thinking directly in terms of what we now call phase space, but the essence of his theories can be expressed in this way.

10. See, for example, B.J.T. Dobbs, *The Foundations of Newton's Alchemy: or, The Hunting of the Greene Lyon* (New York: Cambridge University Press, 1983).

▪ Chapter 2

1. For a popular account of the ideas of superstrings, see F. David Peat, *Superstrings and the Search for a Theory of Everything* (Chicago: Contemporary Books, 1988).

2. Anthony Lee, *Fearful Symmetry: The Search for Beauty in Modern Physics*. (New York: Macmillan, 1988).

3. Roger Penrose's ideas on twistors and twistor geometry are explained in Peat's *Superstrings and the Search for a Theory of Everything*.

▪ Chapter 3

1. A number of books deal with the problems and paradoxes involved in interpreting the quantum theory. Nick Herbert's

Quantum Reality: Beyond the New Physics, (Garden City, New York: Doubleday/Anchor Press, 1985) provides a good introduction. For those who want to go more deeply into these questions, John Archibald Wheeler and Wojciech Hubert Zurek have collected seminal papers by the founders of quantum theory in *Quantum Theory and Measurement* (Princeton, New Jersey: Princeton University Press, 1983).

2. David Bohm and Basil Hiley have proposed what they call a causal interpretation of the quantum theory that does avoid the paradoxes of measurement. But this is not so much an alternative interpretation of an existing formalism as it is a radical revision of the whole ontology of quantum theory—a change in the whole meaning of what a quantum particle actually is. Further details of this novel approach can be found in Chapter 5.

Chapter 4

1. Technical details can be found in the following scientific papers: F. D. Peat, "Time, Structure and Objectivity in Quantum Theory," *Foundations of Physics 18* (1988):1213; idem, "The Evolution of Structure and Order in Quantum Mechanical Systems," *Collective Phenomena*, 2 (1976):149; idem, "The Emergence of Structure and Organization from Physical Systems," *International Journal of Quantum Chemistry: Quantum Biology* Symposium no. 1 (1974), p. 213.

2. Not all physicists agree, however, that the growth of a quasi crystal is directed at the global level.

Chapter 5

1. However, I do not altogether accept the Big Bang convention that the universe was created at a single instant in time. The discussion of the previous chapter suggests that there is no fundamental level or origin to the universe. The "Big Bang radiation" may nonetheless be the residue of some spectacular event occurring within a particular range of energies and space-time.

2. *Electromagnetic Bio-Information*, edited by Fritz-Albert

Popp, Ulrich Warnke, Herbert L. Konig, and Walter Peschka. (Munich-Vienna-Baltimore: Urnab & Schwarzenberg, 1989).

3. Discussion of Bohm's ideas can be found in *Wholeness and the Implicate Order* (London: Routledge & Kegan Paul, 1980) and in *Science, Order and Creativity*, co-authored with F. David Peat (New York: Bantam Books, 1987).

4. C. G. Jung, *Memories, Dreams and Reflections* (New York: Random House, 1967) Fontana Library.

5. G. Fauconnier *Mental Spaces*. See also Alan J. Ford and F. David Peat, "The Role of Language in Science," *Foundations of Physics* 18, 1233 (1988).

▓ Chapter 6

1. Seeing the universe as a symphony or work of art is also explored in F. David Peat, "Mathematics and the Language of Nature" in *Mathematics and Science*, edited by Ronald E. Mickens, (Teaneck, New Jersey: World Scientific, 1990), pp. 154–172.

2. See John S. Bell, *Speakable and unspeakable in quantum mechanics* (New York: Cambridge University Press, 1987). See also F. David Peat, *Einstein's Moon: Bell's Theorem and the Curious Quest for Quantum Reality* (Chicago: Contemporary Books, 1990).

3. Rupert Sheldrake, *A New Science of Life: The Hypothesis of Formative Causation* (London: Blond and Briggs, 1985) and idem, *The Presence of the Past: Morphic Resonance and the Habits of Nature* (New York: Random House/Vintage Books, 1989).

▓ Chapter 7

1. Colin M. Turnbull, *The Forest People*. (New York: Simon and Schuster/Touchstone Books, 1968).

2. See James Glieck, *Chaos Theory: Making a New Science* (New York: Viking, 1987). See also John Briggs and F. David Peat, *The Turbulent Mirror: An Illustrated Guide to Chaos Theory and the Science of Wholeness* (New York: Harper & Row, 1989).

3. Heinz Pagels, *The Dreams of Reason* (New York: Bantam Books, 1988). See also Roger Penrose, *The Emperor's New Mind*

(New York: Oxford University Press, 1989) and F. David Peat, *Artificial Intelligence: How Machines Think* (New York: Baen Books, 1988).

4. Waddington's ideas are discussed in Rupert Sheldrake's *The Presence of the Past: Morphic Resonance and the Habits of Nature.* (New York: Random House/Vintage Books, 1989).

5. A discussion of all these ideas can be found in John Briggs and F. David Peat, *The Turbulent Mirror: An Illustrated Guide to Chaos Theory and the Science of Wholeness* (New York: Harper & Row, 1989).

Chapter 8

1. Joseph W. Meeker, *The Comedy of Survival: In Search of an Environmental Ethic* (Los Angeles, California: Guild of Tutors Press, 1980).

2. There are structures in the hippocampus associated with the functioning of memory, but they seem to have more to do with how memory is processed, stored, and retrieved than with its actual location.

3. Certain of these speculations can be tested experimentally. Currently, artificial intelligence researchers are directing a great deal of attention to neural nets, complex networks used in information processing in which the data that is passing through the net influences the sensitivity of each interconnection. In this way neural nets can be taught to do new tasks and recognize patterns, since repeated input of data cause them to "learn" by modifying their interconnections. It would be interesting to design a system in which these interconnections are also correlated nonlocally. A high degree of very subtle information, or memory, distributed over the whole system, would to influence its performance.

INDEX